RURAL WORKERS' DWEI

CONTENTS

1. INTRODUCTION

Note – This text is prepared on the basis of an understanding of the law and policy as it applied in mid-2014 at a time when significant changes had been made but their effects had largely yet to be tested. In England, the National Planning Policy Framework applied and PPS 7 had been withdrawn. In Wales, TAN 6 (2010) was in force. Scotland had moved to the structure of Scottish Planning Policies and the national Policy Framework, with both revised in 2014. In Northern Ireland, PPS 21 (2010) applied but local plan making was about to be devolved to the new district councils.

1.1   Overview

1.1.1   This paper focuses on the planning framework for agricultural and rural workers' housing under the various development control regimes in the United Kingdom. These matters are generally determined separately in each of England, Wales, Scotland and Northern Ireland with their own legislation, policies and approaches, offering a range of examples that can be mutually instructive. Although England and Wales have to date shared the same statute law for planning, Wales has now used its new powers to issue a Planning Bill while England's localism policy can be used to devolve discretion in widely varied ways within the country. The structure of this paper follows those realities, taking each country in turn.

1.1.2   A largely common theme is that, with the introduction of England's National Planning Policy Framework, there is now no national planning policy statement in Great Britain that provides a specific exception allowing isolated housing for agricultural occupancy. Whether in England, Wales or Scotland all such national policies are now more broadly based on rural workers, rural enterprises and the rural economy. Northern Ireland offers policies for housing for both rural workers and agricultural workers.

1.1.3   While it has been conventional to follow the names of the key statutes in talking in one phrase of both town and country planning, the development control regimes in the United Kingdom have very largely been about settlements, with a general bias towards leaving agriculture and forestry as paramount uses beyond the boundaries of recognised settlements. For policy reasons that shifted over the years, development, and particularly housing, was to be discouraged outside recognised settlements, avoiding uncontrolled and sporadic development. Practicality saw a particular exception evolve for dwellings required for agricultural and forestry workers who might have an essential need to live close to their work.

1.1.4   That category of worker, defined by need, has in practice covered what may be in reality two overlapping sectors:
- labour employed in the enterprise
- the proprietorial needs of the farming family, sometimes seeking a farmhouse.

1.1.5   That approach has broadened to consider other rural enterprises. **Wales** has developed both:
- a general policy in TAN 6 for rural enterprise dwellings and
- One Planet Development, a specifically Low Impact Development policy for applications that enhance (or do not diminish) the environment.

1.1.6   The position in **England** has recently developed radically with the combination of:
- the new National Planning Policy Framework's regime after the withdrawal of PPS7

3

    – the new permitted development rights for agricultural buildings to be converted to dwellings.

The result of these two changes should be reviewed together as it may often be advantageous to secure a full planning permission for a dwelling rather than work within the constrained permitted development rights regime. However, where an applicant has those permitted development rights available that may assist an application for a full permission, at the least providing a fallback.

1.2   General

1.2.1   Since 1947, one thrust of development control regimes in the United Kingdom has been to resist all but the most necessary development (and particularly housing) outside identified settlement boundaries. The particular need for accommodation for agricultural workers (and certain other rural needs) has then been recognised by developing guidance for exceptions to that policy. The first thirty years from the post-war Town and Country Planning Acts saw that guidance steadily developed and formalised, promoting tests and with a standard agricultural occupancy condition ("planning tie" or "ag tag").

1.2.2   Especially over recent years, policy in **England** has tended to become more restrictive on agricultural development from the introduction in 1960 of the 5,000 sq ft (now simply converted to an equivalent $465m^2$) ceiling on the area for permitted development rights for buildings to the rules for intensive livestock buildings in the late 1980s. Similarly, policies and attitudes tightened in respect of agricultural workers' dwellings resulting in the approach of circulars, PPG7 and last recorded in Annexe A of PPS 7, setting functional and financial tests for exceptional permissions with a model form of occupancy condition.

1.2.3   That tide now appears, at least for the moment, to have turned. In practice, approaches to rural development often tended to be more understanding of such applications the further the authority was from London. Now, a series of recent developments have set a new course:
    – new permitted development rights have been given in England for re-using agricultural buildings as warehouses, shops, professional offices, B1 business, restaurants and cafes, hotels, assembly and leisure, schools and nurseries, and now dwellings (see Chapter 6 below)
    – the cancellation of PPS7 and its guidance for agricultural workers' dwellings, all replaced by the new NPPF.

1.2.4   The substantial changes made by the 2010 Coalition government to the development control regime in England have, among many other matters, substantially redrawn the English regime for rural workers' dwellings. The replacement of all existing guidance with the much-reduced National Planning Policy Framework (NPPF) in March 2012 combined with the exposed position of Local Planning Authorities (LPAs) without approved plans has swept away much that had been understood. A major section of this paper explores the new English policy framework to assist members and others with the many questions that arise from the broad principles-based guidance offered by the NPPF in place of the previous detailed central guidance.

1.2.5   The full impact of these changes will only come as applicants, advisers, LPAs, appellants and inspectors come to frame their analysis and arguments in the new terms. As *Embleton* shows, some of that change may require illumination by court decisions.

1.2.6   Many English planning authorities have adopted plans for development control which may also have policies relevant to these issues and will have weight under the new policy framework and its combined emphasis on localism and sustainable development. Some of these plans will pre-date the NPPF, some are more recent and there will also now be more locally driven neighbourhood plans in some areas. This makes it important to understand the local as well as the national policy framework.

1.2.7   Scotland has also moved to broad principles-based planning policy statements with a consolidation of the associated guidance. Rural development policy has generally not been contentious in Scotland in the way that such planning issues can be in England. The Scottish approach to housing outside settlements has rested on the rural economy since at least 2010, with no specific reference to agriculture or forestry. It recommends that, at least in the more remote areas, no occupancy conditions be imposed.

1.2.8   While **Wales** has adopted a national policy statement, Planning Policy Wales, it continues to make specific, detailed and separate provisions for rural workers housing in TAN 6 (2010). While much more in the style of the former English PPS7, this is again a much broader policy for rural workers' dwellings, including provision for dwellings to ease generational succession on farms (though when such dwellings are not needed they are to be part of the local stock of affordable housing). Accordingly, Chapter 7 below on Wales considers TAN 6 in some detail. However, there seems to be only limited experience of its operation which seems to be one of the reasons for the publication of its accompanying Practice Guidance in 2011. The analysis here may help develop confidence in the use of this policy.

1.2.9   Northern Ireland, with its very different rural settlement pattern, has tended to be much more liberal. Subject to constraints on the business, established farms and commercial equestrian operations can secure dwellings without occupancy conditions while rural enterprises may, subject to tests, be given permission but with an occupancy condition.

1.3   Planning Status and Value
1.3.1   Restricting the use of a property may restrict its value, according to the restriction, the circumstances and the market with its current conditions.

1.3.2   Historically, recognising that factor has been an essential part of the marketing commonly required by planning authorities as part of seeking to lift such restrictions. However, recent consumer protection legislation makes it clear that such marketing is bad, indeed illegal, practice where there is no intention to complete any transaction. The potential consumer is being misled and may spend money and effort pointlessly. That may refocus attention on other ways of testing whether the restriction is still appropriate.

1.3.3   Whether it is better seen as a planning obligation or a tax on development, Community Infrastructure Levy (CIL) will be relevant in a growing number of LPAs and so is also discussed.

2. STATUTE LAW ON RURAL WORKERS' DWELLINGS IN ENGLAND AND WALES

2.1   Town and Country Planning Legislation

2.1.1   A comprehensive statutory basis for the administration of development control by local planning authorities within national rules was first laid down as part of the post-war legislation in 1947. The present principal statute for England and Wales is the Town and Country Planning Act 1990 (TCPA), although this has since been amended in several respects. That post-war framework provides that:

- in general, changes in the use of any land or operations, such as building, to any land are subject to planning control, requiring planning permission
- local authorities have the powers for the detailed administration of the development control system within a framework of national policies regulated by an appeal system and the courts.
- these Local Planning Authorities (LPAs) are increasingly required to prepare development plans to set out publicly their local policies.

2.1.2   The basic statutory mechanism is that planning permission is required for any development of land (s.57(1)). "Development" is defined at s.55(1) as

> "the carrying out of building, engineering, mining or other operations in, on, over or under land, or the making of any material change in the use of any buildings or other land".

A critical point is that is that "development" may be making a change of use or operations and works.

2.1.3   S.55(1A), inserted by the Planning and Compensation Act 1991, defines "building operations" to include:

> "(a) demolition of buildings;
> (b)   rebuilding;
> (c)   structural alterations of or additions to buildings; and
> (d)   other operations normally undertaken by a person carrying on business as a builder."

2.1.4   The Act provides its own definition of "land":

> " "land" means any corporeal hereditament, including a building, and, in relation to the acquisition of land under Part IX, includes any interest in or right over land;" (s.336)

(Note: Part IX of the Act deals with powers of compulsory acquisition of land for development purposes, including regeneration schemes.)

2.1.5   If left at that, the system would pose an impossible level of bureaucracy and process over a complex and changing economy and society, which in practice would lead to wide-scale breach. Therefore, exceptions to that requirement have been made:

- in the statute
- by statutory instruments such as the Use Classes Order (accommodating many changes of use between similar uses) and the General Permitted Development Orders (GPDO) giving general permission, usually subject to conditions, qualifications or notification of the proposal to the LPA

while guidance (Circulars, PPGs, PPSs and the like) has been used to bring varying mixes of certainty or simplicity to the system.

2.1.6   The Exception for Agricultural Use – Reflecting the approach of post-war planning policy, the Act specifically states that the **use** of any land for agriculture (or for forestry) is not to be development:

> "The following operations or uses of land shall not be taken for the purposes of this Act to involve development of the land—
>
> ......
>
> (e) the use of any land for the purposes of agriculture or forestry (including afforestation) and the use for any of those purposes of any building occupied together with land so used" (s.55(2)).

2.1.7   Agriculture itself is defined at s.336 of the TCPA:

> " "agriculture" includes horticulture, fruit growing, seed growing, dairy farming, the breeding and keeping of livestock (including any creature kept for the production of food, wool, skins or fur, or for the purpose of its use in the farming of land), the use of land as grazing land, meadow land, osier land, market gardens and nursery grounds, and the use of land for woodlands where that use is ancillary to the farming of land for other agricultural purposes, and "agricultural" shall be construed accordingly".

2.1.8   These are terms close to those used for tenancy legislation and have been the subject of judicial decisions, especially in the context of equestrian uses. Forestry is not defined in the Act. The important point is that this concerns the use of land, not any construction works.

2.1.9   Caravans for Agriculture – That situation has led to the conclusion of the Court of Appeal in *Wealden* regarding the use of caravans on agricultural land. In that case a caravan had been placed on a 15 acre holding to provide both feed storage and accommodation. The Court of Appeal held that this was not operational development but a use of the land and that use was for the purposes of agriculture. Thus, permission was not needed as the use of land for purposes of agriculture is statutorily deemed not to be development. Issues over site licensing for caravans are reviewed briefly below at 5.6.25.

2.2   Separate Policies for England and Wales

2.2.1   Within that overall framework, development control policy for Wales is devolved so that England and Wales each set their own frameworks for planning policy, currently:

  – the National Planning Policy Framework in England
  – Planning Policy Wales.

2.2.2   Until the creation of the Welsh Assembly in 1999, the statutory instruments under these Acts were made by Parliament but, having had the involvement of the Welsh Office, that power was then devolved to the Assembly under the Wales Act 1998 and the National Assembly for Wales (Transfer of Functions Order) 1999.

2.2.3   The effect of that is while the General Permitted Development Order 1995 applies in both England and Wales, changes to it since 1999 will only apply in the country in which they were made. The immediate example of that is that the new permitted development power to convert agricultural buildings introduced in England in April 2014 does not apply in Wales.

2.2.4   Since 2011 Wales has the power to make its own Acts for town and country planning except for matters of national infrastructure. While the Assembly has not yet exercised that power, a Planning (Wales) Bill was published in October 2014.

2.3   National Planning Policy Framework for England

2.3.1   Following the Localism Act, the National Planning Policy Framework (NPPF) was published on 27th March 2012 as a fundamental document setting out planning policies for England. It is to be taken into account when considering planning applications and appeals and when preparing development plans.

2.3.2   The NPPF sets out the Government's general policies for development control. Ministers were clear that they wished to replace over 1,000 pages of guidance with some 50 pages of principles, within which there was to be more discretion. National policy is looking for that discretion to be used positively, especially with widely reported concerns that the planning system was frustrating economic recovery and progress.

2.3.3   Its key statement is the central presumption in favour of sustainable development, encompassing economic, environmental and social sustainability. Paragraph 14 of the NPPF states that the presumption
>   "should be seen as a golden thread running through both plan-making and decision-taking".

2.3.4   The NPPF's specific provisions for housing outside settlements, and so for rural workers' housing, are considered below in Chapter 5.

2.4   Local Development Plans

2.4.1   The legal and policy framework for local development plans has gone through several changes over decades, wrestling with the frequent tendency of the system to be negative in its effects. More recently, the Planning and Compulsory Purchase Act 2004 (PCPA) looked to LPAs to prepare local development frameworks and imposed a requirement to consider sustainability. In their own circumstances, LPAs often made slow progress in doing this but the Act made a general provision that pre-existing plans would cease to have effect by September 2007 unless the Secretary of State made specific direction (Schedule 8, para 1).

2.4.2   The PCPA 2004 tried to assist LPAs with the problems of plan preparation and approval with a portfolio approach, so that only those parts of a local plan which need review have to be considered at any one time. The result is, inevitably, a more complex system with a plethora of different documents and programmes. In summary, it includes:

- The Local Development Scheme (LDS) – the LDS is intended to be a statement of the programme of production of local development documents, setting out which documents are to be prepared and over what timescale. Every local planning authority must prepare and maintain one.
- Local Development Documents (LDDs) – taken as a whole, the LDDs must set out the local authority's policies for land use and development in its area. They can include site allocation policies; statements of objectives for such matters as design, environment or economy; and maps or plans to support policies.
- Statement of Community Involvement (SCI) – the local authority must have a statement which sets out their policy on engaging the local community throughout the local development planning process.

2.4.3   The local plans must go through a process of consultation and independent examination before being submitted to the Secretary of State for approval, after which they can be adopted by the local authority.

2.4.4   The Localism Act 2011, possibly the last statute on general development control to apply to both England and Wales, created an additional option for Local Development Plans, the Neighbourhood Plan. This enables an area within an LPA (and so perhaps, for example, an estate) to set its own very local development control plan, provided certain procedures are followed. Such plans are not to be more onerous than the existing policies. One early example of such a Neighbourhood Plan is that for the Upper Eden area of Cumbria around Brough and Kirkby Stephen whose rural housing policy is noted below and formally recognised as part of Eden District Council's Development Framework on 11th April 2013 after the various stages including a referendum with 90 per cent support from those voting. This Plan's liberal policies for rural housing are reviewed below at 5.2.2.

2.4.5   Interaction Between the NPPF and Local Plans – Paragraphs 208 to 219 of the NPPF review its implementation and so its interaction with local development plans.

2.4.6   The NPPF's policies applied from the day it was published. The operational principle is that:
> "applications for planning permission must be determined in accordance with the development plan unless material considerations indicate otherwise." (Para 210)

2.4.7   Existing local plans "should not be considered out-of-date simply because they were adopted prior to the publication of this Framework" (para 211). "However, the policies contained in this Framework are material considerations which local planning authorities should take into account from the day of its publication. The Framework must also be taken into account in the preparation of plans." (para 212)

2.4.8   A 12 month period of grace was allowed from March 2012 in which authorities might:
> "continue to give full weight to relevant policies adopted since 2004 even if there is a limited degree of conflict with this Framework." (para 214)

2.4.9   In all other cases (and so since March 2013):
> "due weight should be given to relevant policies in existing plans according to their degree of consistency with this framework (the closer the policies in the plan to the policies in the Framework, the greater the weight that may be given)." (para 215).

2.4.10   As the NPPF "aims to strengthen local decision making and reinforce the importance of up-to-date plans (Para 209), its paragraph 213 prompts full or partial reviews of plans to take its policies into account. In that:
> "decision-takers may also give weight to relevant policies in emerging plans according to:
> - the stage of preparation of the emerging plan (the more advanced the preparation, the greater the weight that may be given);
> - the extent to which there are unresolved objections to relevant policies (the less significant the unresolved objections, the greater the weight that may be given); and
> - the degree of consistency of the relevant policies in the emerging plan to the policies in this Framework (the closer the policies in the emerging plan to the policies in the Framework, the greater the weight that may be given)."

2.4.11 Thus, it could be that where a provision in an older plan is in conflict with the NPPF it might, according to the circumstances, be given lesser weight in determining an application.

2.5 Protected Areas and Landscapes

2.5.1 Certain landscapes are protected for planning purposes and different policies and rules apply within them, including Green Belt land, National Parks, Areas of Outstanding Natural Beauty (AONB) and conservation areas. Other sites are protected by designations including Sites of Special Scientific Interest and Scheduled Monuments. Some specific areas have their own status, such as the Norfolk Broads. It can be more difficult to secure approval for development in these areas.

2.5.2 Article 4 Areas – These are defined areas from which an LPA has made a direction withdrawing selected permitted development rights (using what is Article 4 of the Permitted Development Order in each part of the United Kingdom). This usually happens for conservation reasons but is sometimes done to prevent persistent abuse of the system.

2.5.3 Green Belt Land – The designation of land as "Green Belt" is a non-statutory planning policy permitted by each country's main planning legislation implemented by local authorities and included in local plans. In England, its essential purpose has always been, as stated in England's NPPF with an entire chapter on it:

"to prevent urban sprawl by keeping land permanently open".

2.5.4 Green belt policy is to stop cities and towns coalescing into each other, not to prohibit all development. Provided the goal of keeping land open is met, development is not prohibited altogether on Green Belt land. Inappropriate development harmful to the Green Belt is not to be permitted save in very special circumstances that outweigh the harm. The NPPF indicates that certain development would not be inappropriate, including:

- agricultural and forestry buildings (PPS 2 also mentioned agricultural dwellings);
- facilities for outdoor recreation;
- proportionate extensions to existing buildings;
- the redevelopment of existing buildings and limited infilling in existing settlements

Almost of necessity, mineral extraction and transport infrastructure is also deemed not to be inappropriate.

2.5.5 New housing will not generally be acceptable within a Green Belt unless the potential harm to the character of the Green Belt is "clearly outweighed" by the circumstances. The national planning guidance on 'Housing and economic land availability assessment' states:

"Unmet housing need (including for traveller sites) is unlikely to outweigh the harm to the Green Belt and other harm to constitute the "very special circumstances" justifying inappropriate development on a site within the Green Belt."

2.5.6 Scottish policy on green belts (previously in SPP 21) is now set out in Scottish Planning Policy 2014 at paragraphs 49 to 52, allowing local planning authorities to designate land as green belt to support their spatial strategies by:

- "directing development to the most appropriate locations and supporting regeneration;

3. PLANNING CONDITIONS, PLANNING AGREEMENTS AND COMMUNITY INFRASTRUCTURE LEVY

Devolution Note – While the opening to this Chapter has been largely drafted with England and Wales in mind, the position for Wales, Scotland and Northern Ireland is considered at 3.3, 3.4 and 3.5 below and then in Chapters 7, 8 and 9 respectively. However, the common phrasing of many existing agricultural occupancy conditions is likely to mean that the analysis in 3.2 below of the standard English condition may be relevant elsewhere in the United Kingdom.

3.1 Planning Conditions

3.1.1 Conditions are frequently attached to planning consents, including those for agricultural dwellings. These may, for example, include:
- restricting occupation to an agricultural or rural worker only
- making the occupation personal
- limiting the term of the planning consent for a specified period, to make the planning consent temporary and so require a mobile home.

It can be assumed that similar conditions will be developed for permissions for rural workers' housing.

3.1.2 Planning conditions may only be imposed if they meet certain statutory requirements and may be subject to appeal if they do not meet non-statutory tests. Statutory authority for the principle of applying a condition to a planning consent is given by s.70(1) TCPA 1990:

"(1) Where an application is made to a local planning authority for planning permission—
(a) subject to sections 91 and 92, they may grant planning permission, either unconditionally or subject to such conditions as they think fit..."

3.1.3 This is then expanded in s.72(1), which states that conditions may be attached to a planning consent for regulating the development or use of land; or to require the carrying out of works on land; or to require the removal of buildings or works at the end of a specified period.

3.1.4 The courts have considered what reasonable restraints can be placed on the local authority's ability to issue such conditions "as they think fit". In a succession of cases including *Pyx Granite Co Ltd v Ministry of Housing and Local Government* [1958], *Fawcett Properties Ltd v Buckingham County Council* [1961] and *Newbury District Council v Secretary of State for the Environment* [1981], a number of tests have been established to assess the validity of planning conditions. They are now summarised in paragraph 206 of the NPPF:

"Planning conditions should only be imposed where they are necessary, relevant to planning and to the development to be permitted, enforceable, precise and reasonable in all other respects."

That summary restates the six conditions set out in the analysis in former Planning Circular 11/95 drawn from decided cases. Where a condition does not meet these requirements it may be considered ultra vires.

3.1.5 The previous guidance on the use and wording of planning conditions in Circular 11/95 has been replaced by the much briefer guidance, Use of Planning Conditions, published alongside the NPPF on the Planning Portal website. The guidance states that new standard wordings for conditions will be added in due course but these were not available at the time of writing. Appendix A to Circular 11/95, setting out standard wordings for conditions, is still in force at the time of writing.

3.2   Occupancy Restrictions in England

3.2.1   While occupancy conditions linked to agriculture were developed from the early days of the 1947 Act, the principle of using a planning condition to restrict the occupation of a property to those engaged in agriculture was accepted by the House of Lords in *Fawcett Properties Ltd v Buckingham County Council*. In that case, consent had been given for the development of agricultural workers' cottages on Green Belt land, subject to a condition that they could only be occupied by those who were engaged in agriculture, an industry dependent on agriculture, or forestry; or their dependants (so a broader range of occupants than the later conventional definition). The cottages were constructed and later acquired by Fawcett Properties which sought to have the condition removed on the grounds that it was *ultra vires*. The House of Lords held that the condition was fairly and reasonably related to the development.

3.2.2   When agricultural occupancy conditions were first used in the 1950s and 1960s, the wording used by different local authorities could vary considerably – as shown by *Fawcett Properties*. Over time, the wording became more standardised and the Government set out its recommended wording most recently in Appendix A to Circular 11/95 (affirmed in PPS 7 Annex A while it was current):

> "The occupation of the dwelling shall be limited to a person solely or mainly working, or last working, in the locality in agriculture or in forestry, or a widow or widower of such a person, and to any resident dependants."

Local authorities have conventionally followed this wording.

3.2.3   Sometimes an occupancy condition may have been placed on an existing dwelling on the farm as well as or instead of the new one.

3.2.4   As a matter of analysis, the use of the condition turns on "need", not demand; that it is warranted, not just that it is wanted. This point is also material when considering approaches to lifting such conditions.

3.2.5   As the wording used determines the permitted use of the dwelling and can be critical to any prospects for having the condition removed in future, it is always worth carefully checking the actual wording of the condition since:

> – it may be historic and so could be more tolerant in its use
> – some specific point or error may have been made in its drafting.

3.2.6   There can be difficulties in interpreting the standard wording of the condition in the contest of the facts to hand.

3.2.7   **"Mainly" Working** – While it should be relatively straightforward to identify someone who is "solely" working in agriculture, the test for "mainly" working is assessed on the basis that the employment is more than part time. That can require evidence of hours worked throughout the year.

3.2.8   **"Last Working"** – Circular 11/95 gave some guidance on the phrase "last working" at its End Note 4. It was to cover

> "the case both of a person who is temporarily unemployed or of a person who from old age, or illness is no longer able to work. Nor need the words necessarily exclude a person who is engaged in other part-time, or temporary employment, if that person could still be regarded as a farm worker or retired farm worker, or

a worker in one of the other specified categories. (*Fawcett Properties Ltd v Buckingham County Council*). A person who last worked in agriculture/forestry but who now works on a permanent basis mainly in non-agricultural/forestry employment, would not satisfy model condition 45."

Thus, where someone who is retired or no longer working then starts work again outside agriculture, that could be in breach of the occupancy condition.

3.2.9   **"Locality"** – The definition of "locality" is likely to vary depending on the type of farm and the area in which it is located. "Locality" might refer to a smaller geographical area for a livestock farm than for an arable unit, for example, if it could be shown that arable workers were generally prepared to travel longer distances to work. As a word and without further definition, "locality" may risk being void for uncertainty. Its interpretation may be coloured by the immediate context as such matters as whether it is judged by travel time or distance (for example, South Somerset is understood to take 10 kilometres (6.23 miles) as a distance for guidance). While some authorities took the view that the locality could not go beyond their boundaries, this is not seen as relevant. The concept has also been considered in the context of attempts by planning authorities to impose local occupation conditions on housing where it has been challenged for uncertainty.

3.2.10   **"Resident Dependants"** – This expression might often refer to children, non-earning spouses or elderly parents. End Note 5 to Circular 11/95 commented that the phrase means:

> "persons living in family with the person defined and dependent on him (or her) in whole or in part for their subsistence and support (Fawcett Properties Ltd v Buckingham County Council [1961] A.C. 636 at page 671)."

That may therefore on occasion raise an issue where a person in the dwelling is not dependent on the worker (as perhaps by being the higher earner) though this may often be answered by 11/95's reference to "dependent on him (or her) in whole or in part".

3.2.11   That point has now been considered by the High Court in *Shortt* where the court dismissed a claim that the occupation of a property was in contravention of an agricultural occupancy condition because the farmer's husband and children were not financially dependent on her farming income.

3.2.12   Mrs Shortt farmed about 55 acres of land in Worcestershire from a house built in 1975 and subject to the following agricultural occupancy condition:

> "The occupation of the dwelling shall be permitted to persons employed or last employed solely or mainly and locally in agriculture as defined by section 290(1) of the Town and Country Planning Act 1971, or in forestry and the dependants (which shall be taken to include a widow or widower) of such persons."

She kept a few beef cattle but had made no profits for many years. Her husband had his own career which supported the family financially. In September 2012, Mrs Shortt applied for a certificate of lawfulness of use or development for continued use of the property without compliance with the occupancy condition, on the ground that her husband and children had resided in the property without being her "dependants" for more than 10 years, relying on the decision in *Fawcett*.

3.2.13   However, the court found that there was no single definition of "dependant" which is applicable in all circumstances and noted

> "…so far as the definition of "dependant" is concerned, context is everything"

and considered that the statutory context here from which the term "dependants" arose did not necessarily imply financial dependency, concluding:

> "…the words as used in the Planning Condition, looked at as a whole, appear to

15

me to envisage "dependency" in a wider and more open-textured way than one requiring an element of financial dependency, certainly to include a spouse and minor children of the worker who is their wife and mother and who provides them with usual family services and care."

As a result, Mr Shortt and the children could be considered to be dependants under this wider definition and so the property had not been occupied in breach of the condition.

3.2.14 LPAs may seek to use an agreement under s.106 (previously s.52) to link one or both dwellings to the holding so that no houses can be sold away separately.

3.3 Occupancy Restrictions in Wales (see also 7.6 below)

3.3.1 Until the introduction in 2010 of the Rural Enterprise Dwellings policies of TAN6, Wales shared the same policies as England in regard to agricultural dwellings. The new model rural enterprise occupancy condition (as revised in 2011) is discussed in detail at section 7.6 below. The point to note here is that where the occupancy condition cannot be satisfied by a qualifying rural enterprise worker, the property is then to be available to those qualifying for affordable housing.

3.3.2 Wales issued its own Circular 16/2014 in October 2014 to offer official guidance on the use of planning conditions, replacing Welsh Office Circular 35/95 (the equivalent of the English Circular 11/95). That gives guidance on the use of conditions in general, providing model forms for many conditions, and on individual conditions, including one for rural enterprise occupation.

3.4 Occupancy Restrictions in Scotland (see also 8.3 below)

3.4.1 Scotland had a very similar approach to agricultural occupancy restrictions to those in England and Wales (albeit in practice perhaps often operated more liberally). However, a letter issued by the Scottish Government's Director and Chief Planner to the local authority Heads of Planning on 4th November 2011 stated in bold type that:

"The Scottish Government believes that occupancy restrictions are rarely appropriate and so should generally be avoided".

It affirmed that "Scottish Planning Policy ... does not promote the use of occupancy restrictions." Where the council is satisfied that there is an adequate land management or business case "it should not be necessary to use formal mechanisms to restrict occupancy". A more restrictive approach might be justified in areas at risk of suburbanisation or to contain long distance commuting. This approach puts the onus on the planning authority to justify using a condition.

3.4.2 A planning authority may also seek to use an agreement under s.75 (previously s.50) to link the new dwelling to the holding so that it cannot be sold away separately. Councils have also used them to regulate occupation, seeing them as less problematic than conditions and not susceptible to appeal. It is now possible that the owner of the land who originally entered into such a planning agreement may remain liable for implementing its terms even after selling the affected land.

3.4.3 It may be noted that some councils such as Stirling, feeling under development pressure, responded to the Chief Planner's letter by looking to use conditions rather than agreements.

3.5 Occupancy Restrictions in Northern Ireland

3.5.1 While some properties are subject to agricultural occupancy conditions from before 2010, PPS 21 does not require an occupancy conditions for a dwelling on a farm business with a six year history. The policies of PPS21 operate instead to limit the flexibility of the business as to location and further dwellings.

3.5.2   Occupancy conditions are to be imposed for dwellings for other established enterprises in open country and where the dwelling is warranted by personal circumstances.

3.6   Occupancy Restrictions and Value

3.6.1   An occupancy restriction limits who may lawfully occupy and so use the property (though not who may own it). Limiting the use of a property can limit its value though the extent of that will turn on circumstances.

3.6.2   As a practical matter, it is now very difficult to secure a mortgage on a property subject to an agricultural occupancy condition. That restricts the market of purchasers (and those subsequent purchasers for future onward sales who give the current buyer an exit route) to those with either sufficient available funds to buy without a mortgage or with other assets that are acceptable as security. With the substantial support given by mortgage finance to large areas of the housing market that is a significant factor. It is noteworthy that in operating its policy in PPS 21 for dwellings needed for personal circumstances with an associated occupancy condition, the Northern Ireland Government has had to issue a letter of comfort to the Council of Mortgage Lenders. The Scottish Chief Planner's letter of November 2011 explained that part of the background to withdrawing general support for the use of occupancy restrictions was the difficulty with mortgages and sales.

3.6.3   It has yet to be seen whether rural worker/enterprise occupancy conditions with a wider range of potential users may attract some lender interest, albeit perhaps at lower loan to value ratios than in the market for unencumbered property.

3.6.4   There is a conventional view that the effect of a typical occupancy condition is to devalue a dwelling by 30 per cent from its unencumbered value. It has also been suggested that the effect of the condition equates to the value of a plot without the condition. On that basis, the dwelling's value might be that of an equivalent unconstrained dwelling reduced by that plot value. These views inter-relate with the expectations of LPAs as to the discounts at which a property should be offered to test the market for available compliant occupiers.

3.6.5   These are no more than rules of thumb, perhaps more appropriate in some circumstances than others, and have no particular authority. For clarity of analysis, the value of a property with an occupancy condition is its market value with the condition. That need not sit in any formal relationship to the unencumbered market value but falls to be assessed in its own right. Discussion of discounts is a practical and colloquial shorthand which needs to be tempered by that understanding. Specific thought should be given to the issue for each case in hand. Even in the same market conditions, the answer may also vary between different local planning authority areas as known differing attitudes towards enforcing or lifting conditions may inform the real market.

3.6.6   In exploring this topic, the CAAV undertook a survey in 2005 of agricultural property sales subject to severe user restrictions, generally precluding further or any development, either directly or by clawback and equivalent provisions. These appeared relevant to sales of agricultural property. Reported in the June 2005 News Letter, this covered 60 transactions from the previous two years and assessed the impact of restrictions in the then market
  – **Interest:** In 73% of cases the restriction was held to have a negligible impact on interest, and an adverse effect in the remaining 27%.
  – **Price:** Respondents reported that the restriction generally had little impact on the price compared with that expected for the property had it been unencumbered 93 per cent reporting no appreciable impact.

17

3.6.7   Further evidence sought of the effect of an agricultural occupancy condition on the value of dwellings suggested a very varied pattern such that in strong markets, dwellings near conurbations might not see any identifiable discount to market value. While in some weaker markets, discounts larger than 30 per cent may be cited for some areas, it might be that at times when both the wider economy and agricultural fortunes were depressed, such properties are not at an identifiable discount but effectively unsaleable.

3.6.8   Not only is the actual figure likely to vary with general factors such as location and the state of the market but it is also important to take account of any factors that may anyway be inherent in the property which may anyway affect its market value without the condition – such as being sited within a working farmstead. In such matters, this issue may be seen as similar to the assessment of "agricultural value" for Agricultural Property Relief from Inheritance Tax (see 3.7.4 below).

3.6.9   This question influences the value at which a local authority might suggest that a dwelling be marketed to test the demand for it when considering an application to lift an occupancy condition. The problems with that approach are discussed in the next chapter but it may be noted here that the grant of the condition turns on need, not demand.

3.7   Agricultural Occupancy Conditions and Taxation
3.7.1   While discussion may often focus on the value at which such properties might be offered for sale when seeking to lift a condition, these issues are also relevant for other matters such as taxation. It may be important to identify the valuation unit, whether it is just the dwelling or there is a larger property of which the dwelling forms a part.

3.7.2   In those occasional cases where an occupancy restriction is accepted on an existing dwelling it may be likely to reduce its value.

3.7.3   For **Council Tax**, an occupancy restriction is likely to be accepted as reducing the value of an affected dwelling, possibly by enough to change the band to which it would otherwise be allocated though its market value may anyway be influenced by the immediate circumstances, such as location in a working farmstead. Further, where the dwelling is part of a larger property in one occupation it will be part of composite hereditament with a need for an apportionment of the value of the whole between the dwelling and the remainder. It is thus possible that a dwelling with a restriction that is part of composite property may be more than one band lower than it would be if it were separately owned and unrestricted. A similar effect would apply to **rateable values in Northern Ireland**.

3.7.4   For Agricultural Property Relief from **Inheritance Tax**, the fact of an occupancy restriction is relevant as a circumstance in which the agricultural value of a property may be the same as its market value. S.115(3) of the Inheritance Tax Act presumes that a covenant limiting the use of the property to "agricultural property" is a permanent one. More generally, a lower value will reduce the size of the taxable estate but set a correspondingly lower base value for Capital Gains Tax in the hands of the heirs. Approaches to that will vary with the parties' circumstances and intentions.

3.7.5   For **Capital Gains Tax** the value of the dwelling is irrelevant where it qualifies as the taxpayer's principal private residence. Otherwise, expenditure in lifting the restriction should be a deductible cost when calculating any relevant gain. Accepting a restriction might reduce or remove any gain.

3.7.6   With the growing array of taxes, including the **Annual Tax on Enveloped Dwellings** (ATED), on higher value dwellings owned by companies and other non-natural persons to apply to dwellings worth over £500,000 (from 1st April 2016), any effect of an occupancy restriction on value may affect liability to them. HMRC's guidance that an average of 20 hours a week work in farming is a practical test for the farmhouse relief from ATED could be consistent with an occupancy condition based on "solely or mainly working in agriculture".

3.7.7   The same will apply where the market value of a house is relevant to the assessment of the occupier's benefits in kind for **Income Tax**.

3.8   Planning Agreements and Obligations

3.8.1   Statute law makes it possible to make a planning permission subject to a legal agreement being put in place between the LPA and the applicant. For England and Wales, the power is given by s.106 of the TCPA 1990 (previously s.52 of the TCPA 1971). For Scotland it is s.75 of the Town and Country Planning (Scotland) Act 1997 and in Northern Ireland Article 40 of the Planning (Northern Ireland) Order 1991. These provide for the developer (in this case, the applicant) to make a legally enforceable commitment to the LPA on measures to make the impact of a development acceptable.

3.8.2   In their original form, these were bilateral agreements so that, while a planning condition can be challenged or lifted, such an agreement could only be varied by agreement. In an agricultural context, a planning agreement may often be used to tie the ownership of the dwelling to the ownership of the farmland that supported its application. While the LPA can feel that helps protect the policy purpose of the permission given and limit its fears of subsequent abuse, that can lead to practical issues where some land needs to be sold or the business restructures. The *Rasbridge* case noted at 4.8.5-13 below concerned an agreement that imposed an occupancy restriction.

3.8.3   In 1991, s.106 was re-cast by the Planning and Compensation Act to introduce planning obligations so that any person interested in land may, by agreement or otherwise, enter into a planning obligation. Such an obligation can be volunteered by the applicant or other qualifying party and need not have the contractual agreement of the LPA. Such a unilateral offer might be made to assist an appellant's prospects at a planning appeal. Under s.106, obligations can:
- restrict the development or use of the land in any specified way
- require specified operations or activities to be carried out in, on, under or over the land
- require the land to be used in any specified way
- require a sum or sums to be paid to the LPA.

They can be registered as a land charge.

3.8.4   The NPPF, replacing the larger provisions of Circular 05/2005, advises at paragraphs 204 and 205 that, in **England**:

"Planning obligations should only be sought where they meet all of the following tests:
- necessary to make the development acceptable in planning terms;
- directly related to the development; and
- fairly and reasonably related in scale and kind to the development.

"Where obligations are being sought or revised, local planning authorities should take account of changes in market conditions over time and, wherever appropriate, be sufficiently flexible to prevent planned development being stalled."

3.8.5   More generally at paragraph 173:
"Pursuing sustainable development requires careful attention to viability and costs in plan-making and decision-taking. Plans should be deliverable. Therefore, the sites and the scale of development identified in the plan should not be subject to such a scale of obligations and policy burdens that their ability to be developed viably is threatened. To ensure viability, the costs of any requirements likely to be applied to development, such as requirements for affordable housing, standards, infrastructure contributions or other requirements should, when taking account of the normal cost of development and mitigation, provide competitive returns to a willing land owner and willing developer to enable the development to be deliverable."

3.8.6   On 28th November 2014, DCLG announced that, for England:
– s.106 obligations should not be used to require affordable housing contributions or other "tariff-style contributions" from developments of less than 10 houses (including self-build, extensions and annexes)
– in areas designated under s.157 of the Housing Act 1985 (areas where rural concerns led to the re-sale of right to buy housing being restricted, including National Parks and AONBs) LPAs can reduce this threshold to 5 units or less
though these changes are not to apply to rural exception sites for affordable housing justified by need. DCLG is to publish revised guidance.

3.8.7   For **Wales**, Planning Policy Wales (July 2014) considers planning obligations and Community Infrastructure Levy in the same section. It states at its 3.71
"Planning obligations are useful arrangements to overcome obstacles which may otherwise prevent planning permission from being granted. Contributions from developers may be used to offset negative consequences of development, to help meet local needs, or to secure benefits which will make development more sustainable. It is essential that arrangements are fair to both the developer and the community, that the process is as transparent as possible, and that development plans provide guidance on the types of obligations which authorities may seek from developers. When granting planning permission local planning authorities may seek to enter into a planning obligation with a developer to:
• restrict development or use of the land;
• require operations or activities to be carried out in, on, under or over the land;
• require the land to be used in a specified way; or
• to require payments to be made to the authority either in a single sum or periodically.

3.8.8   Planning Policy Wales further advises at its 3.7.10 that
"Planning obligations should only be sought where they are necessary to make a proposal acceptable in land use planning terms. Planning permission may not be bought or sold and negotiations should be conducted in a way that is seen to be fair, open and reasonable. Unacceptable development should never be allowed because of unrelated benefits. Acceptable development should never be refused simply because an applicant is unwilling to offer such benefits. If there is a choice between imposing conditions and entering into a planning obligation, the imposition of a condition is preferable. Conditions are more transparent, offer greater flexibility in the light of changing circumstances and offer a developer the right of appeal to the Welsh Ministers against those conditions considered to be onerous."

3.8.9   Breaches of an obligation or agreement are contractual ones and so susceptible to contractual enforcement against the person who made the commitment and their successors in title. S.106(5) allows a restriction or requirement under an obligation to be enforced by an injunction. S.106(6) permits the LPA to enter land to carry out operations subject to the obligation that have not been carried out and recover its costs.

3.8.10   Pre-1991 agreements under s.106 were enforceable as restrictive covenants and can be discharged or modified by the Upper Tribunal (Lands Chamber) – formerly the Lands Tribunal – under s.84 of the Law of Property Act 1925 – again see the *Rasbridge* case at 4.8.5-13 below for an example of an agricultural occupancy agreement challenged in this way.

3.8.11   The approach now to lifting or modifying obligations is discussed at 4.8 below.

3.8.12   Similar amendments were later made to s.75 in Scotland with further discussion in Chapter 8 below.

3.8.13   In practice, some LPAs may prove to be content to waive old agreements where they feel they are time spent but without such mutual agreement they can only be modified by recourse to Tribunal or appeal.

3.8.14   With advent of the Community Infrastructure Levy in England and Wales, a s.106 agreement can only be used to achieve site specific objectives related to the development.

3.9   Community Infrastructure Levy
3.9.1   The Community Infrastructure Levy (CIL) was introduced by the Community Infrastructure Levy Regulations 2010 under the Planning Act 2008 as a charge which local authorities in England and Wales can elect to levy on development within their area in order specifically to fund "infrastructure" in and outside their areas. The definition of "infrastructure" is very broad and can encompass green space, police facilities, schools and hospitals as well as roads, cycle paths and community halls.

3.9.2   Where it is due, CIL must be paid before a planning permission can be lawfully implemented.

3.9.3   Before it can levy a CIL charge, a local authority must issue a draft charging schedule and hold a public consultation. The CIL is usually charged on a £ per unit area basis and may vary for different types of development within the local authority area. In this way, the local authority can encourage certain types of development by levying a lower CIL charge or add to the cost of other types.

3.9.4   The charge is made whenever development creates an increase in floor area and can therefore apply to extensions as well as new build. Smaller developments under 100 square metres will normally be exempt from the charge.

3.9.5   The Self-Build Exemption – An exemption from CIL has been provided to encourage individuals to build or extend their own houses. It is available to anybody who is building their own home or has commissioned a home from a contractor, house builder or sub-contractor. The dwelling must then be owned and occupied by that person as their principal residence for at least three years after the work is completed (or the levy becomes due).

3.9.6   The exemption must be claimed and approved before the work has commenced with the supporting evidence provided on completion (including any of the VAT refund claim by self-build housing, a self-build warranty providing latent defects insurance or a self-build mortgage). Applying requires completion of both an Assumption of Liability form and a Self-Build Exemption Claim – Part 1 form. Before commencing the development, the applicant must also submit a Commencement Notice to the charging authority.

4. LIFTING AN OCCUPANCY CONDITION IN ENGLAND AND WALES

Note: This chapter can only be a brief guide to what can be a long and challenging process and it may be necessary to take expert advice relating to the specific circumstances in hand. While drafted for the situation in England and Wales where these issues appear most contentious in practice, this review will be relevant to equivalent cases in Scotland and Northern Ireland

As reviewed below, the arguments may now have changed:
- *in England, with the introduction of the NPPF and the new Planning Practice Guidance*
- *in Wales, with the alternative of the Rural Enterprise Dwelling Condition.*

4.1   The Position to Date

4.1.1   Someone wishing to have an agricultural occupancy condition removed (or modified) can apply to the LPA to determine that the condition is no longer deemed necessary, often relying on changes in circumstances. If that is refused, then the matter can be taken to appeal for decision by a planning inspector. Issues of law may be referable to the courts.

4.1.2   However, the process is often a difficult one because local authorities must be persuaded that the house, which was probably only given planning consent on the grounds that it was required for an agricultural worker, is genuinely no longer required for that purpose. Further, the wording of most modern occupancy conditions (see 3.2.2) is such that the issue has to be proven for the locality generally and not just in relation to the particular holding.

4.1.3   If a local authority becomes aware of a failure to comply with an agricultural occupancy condition, it can serve a Breach of Condition Notice on the person who has control over the land (s.187A TCPA 1990). The local authority must allow at least 28 days for the person to comply with the notice. There is no right of appeal against such a notice – any challenge would have to be by way of a judicial review. Failure to comply with a Breach of Condition Notice is an offence.

4.1.4   An agricultural occupancy condition can be "lifted" in one of two ways:
- first, by applying for the removal of the occupancy condition. If successful, the condition will be removed from the planning consent and the property is then unburdened. This is the more secure outcome but usually more difficult to achieve.
- second, if the property can be shown to have been occupied in breach of the condition for ten years, then an application can be made for a Certificate of Lawfulness of Existing Use or Development (CLEUD). If successful, this has the effect of preventing enforcement action being taken against an occupier who does not comply with the condition. As this only gives immunity from enforcement action and not a full permission, this is less satisfactory as a solution. Any future occupation by a person who complies with the condition could mean that the Certificate would fall. It is usual to follow a CLEUD with an application for an unqualified permission to secure the wider occupation rights and so value.

4.1.5   A further option to consider is whether an application under s.73 of the 1990 Act for a determination of an application to develop land without compliance with conditions previously attached might be appropriate. The equivalent power in Scotland is under s.42

of the 1997 Act and in Northern Ireland under s.54 of the 2011 Act. That would leave the original planning permission in place (and so protected) but would only consider the question of the conditions and it is not to become more onerous. Overall, it may often be thought more desirable to have the condition lifted than to have it replaced or modernised.

4.1.6   The permission might also be modified by an application. It may be possible to secure LPA agreement to the temporary relaxation of the condition to allow estate cottages that are not currently likely to be needed for farmworkers so that they can lawfully be let on shortholds to a wider market. The LPA retains control, while recognising practicality.

4.1.7   There might also be cases where the applicant would accept a new rural worker condition in place of an old agricultural occupancy condition.

4.1.8   For all these options, it is worth considering meeting a planning officer for pre-application advice, verifying the authority's requirements and policies and reviewing issues.

4.2   Applying for Removal of a Condition

4.2.1   The most obvious cases will be those where the circumstances of the original permission have now changed completely. For example, development may mean that the dwelling is no longer in open country but now surrounded by other unconstrained housing. If no other factors require the retention of the condition, it has become redundant or obsolete.

4.2.2   Such cases may be relatively rare. The more usual situation is one requiring close appraisal of the circumstances to demonstrate that the condition is no longer apt. The LPA has its duties to current public policies on land use to test that proposition and are fully aware of the extent to which the value and utility that may be at stake can drive applicants.

4.2.3   Local authorities will expect to see detailed evidence to support an application for the lifting of an occupancy restriction. Some will have their own particular guidance, but in most cases the applicant will be required to demonstrate that there is no longer a justification for that particular condition to be attached to that particular property.

4.2.4   How Does the Condition Limit the Occupancy? The applicant should start by considering the wording of the condition itself. Older conditions may have non-standard or more liberal wording. This should be carefully considered in the context of the planning consent for the dwelling and any other planning conditions which may be attached. In particular, it is necessary to consider whether the condition applies to the holding only, or to the wider locality, or to some other geographic area. This will dictate the nature of the evidence that the applicant will need to produce to be successful. If the condition refers to an undefined area such as "the locality" then it may be useful to discuss with the planning officers how that should be defined, to minimise the chances of the evidence being dismissed as insufficient because it has not considered demand from a large enough area.

4.2.5   There has been some judicial consideration of the underlying approach in deciding an application to lift a condition. In *Federated Estates*, the High Court observed that:

> "... the term "burden of proof" as it was used in civil litigation between parties was not appropriate in the context of planning appeals. The decision which section 36(3) of the [then] Act required the Secretary of State to take was a decision in the public interest."

23

That approach was then affirmed by the Court of Appeal in *Millbank*. However, an Inspector can only take that decision on the basis of his findings as to the evidence, from his inspection and with his experience and judgment. In that, the appellant is most likely to be the person most interested in marshalling and submitting evidence and argument to demonstrate that the condition is no longer needed. It was the Inspector's apparent errors in understanding the import of those cases that led to a decision lifting an agricultural condition being overturned by the Court in *Lliw Valley Borough Council v Secretary of State for Wales and Evans*.

4.3   Marketing and the Problems with Marketing

4.3.1   The most difficult issue to address is how to respond to the common insistence (despite points above) by the local planning authority that the applicant demonstrate that there is a lack of demand for that type of accommodation from those employed or last employed in agriculture. The point has been made that the real test here should be that of whether there is a need for an agricultural occupancy condition on that dwelling (in its location), not of demand for it. Marketing can only test demand, not need. The problems with marketing a property when there is no intention to sell it are discussed below. Again, it is advisable to discuss this with the planning officers in advance and agree a strategy with them.

4.3.2   Marketing? – The common traditional approach required by local planning authorities has been to test the market for potential occupiers by offering the property for sale or to let with marketing over an agreed period with appropriate advertising, often on a basis agreed with the LPA.

4.3.3   Alongside the required marketing effort, it will usually be expected that the property must be offered at a discounted price to reflect the condition. Experience is that LPAs (and Inspectors) will typically expect to see the property offered at a discount of 25 to 30 per cent from market value – subsequent disputes may turn on this figure. In *R (Epping Forest DC) v STLR and Emery* it was accepted that a 25 per cent discount from an unencumbered value was appropriate. It referred to the asking price being just a "guide"; it was open to any interested person to make an offer at a lower price.

4.3.4   That approach turns on the unfettered market value being fairly assessed. Some LPAs will now ask for three appraisals of the unencumbered market value and then judge the discount it will view as reasonable from an average of those.

4.3.5   The Welsh Government offered its thought on value in the Practice Guidance to TAN 6 – see 7.6.22 below.

4.3.6   For this approach to work, it will naturally be necessary for the applicant to ensure good records of:
- copies of advertisements
- details of enquiries – a Tribunal criticism in *Rasbridge* (noted at 4.8.5-13 below) was that no details had been kept of telephone enquiries that did not result in viewings
- details of viewings
- details of offers received.

It would be relevant to know for each serious expression of interest whether the person appeared compliant with the condition or not. Even serious interest from non-compliant people may not be pertinent demand but rather aid the case for the condition not being relevant.

4.3.7   That will then be submitted to the local authority with the application to lift the condition. This approach may still be an appropriate option *provided* that the property owner is genuinely prepared to sell or let the property if a realistic offer is made. In practice, this may often have been limited to offering the property for sale but there may be a growing interest in whether there would be rental interest in it.

4.3.8   The Problems with Marketing – While the marketing exercise has become conventional, it poses a number of problems. A fundamental one is that the real issue over the condition is whether it is necessary, not whether there is a demand for the property. The two are not identical and not all bidders that may come forward in response to the marketing may say if they qualify under the condition or need the property.

4.3.9   However, where the property owner wishes to keep the property for their own use and does not plan to sell or let it, then it is not appropriate to use the marketing approach to test the market as this would be contrary to the Consumer Protection from Unfair Trading Regulations 2008 (which have replaced the Property Misdescriptions Act). The Regulations prohibit unfair commercial practices which might affect the "transactional decision making" of the average consumer. "Unfair commercial practices" includes making a misleading omission and it seems likely that failing to make clear that a property is not, in fact, available to buy or rent would be a misleading omission which would affect a consumer's decision about whether to proceed with a transaction. A breach of the Consumer Protection Regulations is punishable by a fine and in serious cases, up to two years' imprisonment. The equivalent regulations for businesses are the Business Protection from Misleading Marketing Regulations 2008.

4.3.10   This point had previously been identified by the Inspector in *Lliw Valley* in 1992 when he observed (albeit with his error on the onus of proof):
> "… I accept that it would be unreasonable to expect you to carry out a marketing exercise to show a lack of demand, when you had no intention of selling, since this might be regarded as a fraudulent exercise."

4.3.11   The guidance issued by the former Office of Fair Trading on the 2008 regulations (OFT Guidance on Property Sales – Compliance with Consumer Protection from Unfair Trading Regulations 2008 and the Business Protection from Misleading Marketing Regulations 2008 – September 2012) said:
> "The new regulations ban traders in all sectors from using unfair commercial practices towards consumers. They set out broad rules outlining when commercial practices are unfair. These fall into four main categories [including]:
> - A general ban on conduct below a level which may be expected towards consumers (honest market practice/good faith). This is intended to act as a "safety net" protection for all consumers.
> - Misleading practices, like false or deceptive messages, or leaving out important information. …
>
> For a practice to be unfair under these rules, they must harm, or be likely to harm, the economic interests of the average consumer. For example, when a shopper makes a purchasing decision he or she would not have made had he or she been given accurate information or not put under unfair pressure to do so."

This guidance appears to challenge any LPA insistence on inviting offers for a property that is not really for sale or let. Among the 31 practices specifically identified as banned is
> "**10. Promoting a product you don't want to sell**
> Making an invitation to purchase products at a specified price and then:
> (a) Refusing to show the advertised item to consumers;
> **or**
> (b) Refusing to take orders for it or deliver it within a reasonable time; …"

4.3.12   If a marketing exercise is inappropriate, then it may be necessary to explain to the LPA the applicant's reasons for not being willing to sell or let the dwelling. The LPA's essential concern is with land use policy not the preferences of the applicant.

4.4   Other Approaches

4.4.1   Other evidence which might help to demonstrate a lack of demand (or indeed need) for agricultural workers' dwellings in the area might include:

- a review of the general demand for housing in the area
- a review of the changing nature of agriculture in the locality since the property became subject to the condition. The agricultural workforce has reduced substantially over recent decades with changing enterprises, greater efficiency and use of machinery. There may now be little non-family employment in many areas. However, that may mean there are still potential occupiers who still qualify as retired from agriculture.
- an assessment of the number of rural workers employed in the area at the current time, compared to the number employed when the property became subject to the condition
- details of any new rural workers' dwellings made subject to occupancy conditions over, say, the last five years
- details of any other restricted properties being sold or advertised for sale or to let in the locality over, say, the last five years. Even if the LPA suggests that locality may be narrowly defined it may be prudent to consider a larger area lest it become an issue at any appeal.

4.4.2   Past applications can be sought through the planning register and then investigated to identify their circumstances. The case for such applications is often site-specific and so may not meet the needs of other possible occupiers with their site-specific needs.

4.4.3   It will commonly be the case that when a dwelling is needed, its location in relation to the business is paramount but the historic condition then allows occupation by qualifying workers in a wider area. Yet many of them will need to be very near their work.

4.5   Have The Issues Now Changed in England?

4.5.1   The English planning policy framework for agricultural occupancy conditions has been withdrawn. At the time of writing there is insufficient experience to know what this might mean.

4.5.2   Not only has the new Rural Workers' Housing exception been created by the NPPF but PPS7 with its Annexe A has been withdrawn and the body of Circular 11/95 with its justification for agricultural occupancy conditions was withdrawn in March 2014 with the launch of the Planning Practice Guidance suite.

4.5.3   Appendix A to 11/95 does remain in force to retain the wording of a large number of model conditions under the heading "Suggested Models of Acceptable Conditions for Use in Appropriate Circumstances". Thus, while the template for an agricultural occupancy condition survives, the justification for it in the body of Circular 11/95 has been withdrawn.

4.5.4   As noted, some adopted local plans will however have agricultural occupancy policies, perhaps requiring consideration of the interaction between them and the NPPF in the circumstances to hand.

4.5.5   It is possible that review of an agricultural occupancy condition could see a proposal for its replacement by the rural workers' condition. There may be an analogy in the suggestion in the Welsh TAN 6 that an application to lift an agricultural occupancy condition in Wales might lead to replacing it with a Welsh rural enterprise dwelling condition.

4.5.6   Recent Practical Experience – A review of appeal decisions since the NPPF was introduced in March 2012 (for which we are grateful to David Collier) suggests that there may not yet have been any significant changes in the way agricultural workers' dwelling applications, and applications for removal of agricultural occupancy conditions, are being handled. That review suggests that Inspectors:

   a) will attach significant weight to development plan policies that are consistent with the NPPF and incorporate the tests of PPS7 Annex A (see, for example, APP/C3430/A/12/2185660, decision dated 20th March 2013);
   b) are prepared (indeed very willing) to treat the PPS7 tests as a material consideration even where they are not incorporated into a development plan policy (see, for example, APP/E2530/A/12/2180014, decision dated 29th January 2013, APP/P1133/A/12/2188539, decision dated 17th May 2013, and APP/F2605/A/13/2201606, decision dated 31st December 2013);
   c) will normally make use of the model condition in Circular 11/95 when an agricultural worker's dwelling is approved, rather than a broader restriction (see, for example, APP/K3415/A/13/2206203, decision dated 6th February 2014);
   d) will devise a bespoke condition based on that in 11/95 when a business combines agriculture and other enterprises, such as an equine business (see, for example, APP/H0738/A/13/2193698, decision dated 4th September 2013);
   e) tend to attach very specific occupancy conditions when a dwelling is permitted in connection with a rural business other than a farm, and, because of the uncommon nature of such businesses, tie occupancy to the business in question rather than businesses of that type in the locality; and
   f) are not taking a significantly more liberal approach to applications for the removal of agricultural occupancy conditions (see, for example, APP/Q9495/A/13/2194894, decision dated 20th September 2013).

4.5.7   Much of this may, of course, turn on how the appellants and LPAs presented their cases. Many (like the objectors in *Embleton* and, indeed the parties in the Lands Tribunal case, *Rasbridge*, noted at 4.8.5-13 below) may have defaulted to the arguments of PPS7 rather than those of the NPPF. Without new arguments before them, Inspectors may have been unwilling to break new ground. It may, therefore, be some time before we see if these arguments still usually apply in the new policy world or how far they have changed with the NPPF (and perhaps indeed also with the new permitted development rights reviewed in Chapter 6).

4.6   Has the Issue Now Changed in Wales?
4.6.1   Again, the policy framework for agricultural occupancy conditions has been replaced in Wales by the policies of PPW and TAN 6. The planning policy framework for agricultural occupancy conditions as set out in Circular 11/95 (jointly issued by the Department of the Environment and the Welsh Office) appears to have been withdrawn in Wales – it is not on the list of current circulars on the Welsh Government website.

4.6.2   That situation may suggest that there is no ground for resisting applications for their removal.

4.6.3   The section of TAN 6 that outlines the model Rural Enterprise Dwelling condition concludes by suggesting that it could be used as an answer to applications to lift an agricultural occupancy condition.

4.6.4   It should be noted that that outcome would:
- – accommodate a wider range of workers in rural enterprises than just those in agriculture or forestry
- – where no such worker was available to occupy it, make the dwelling part of the affordable housing provision.

4.6.5   With the pressures on rural society and housing, there may be arguments for discussing with the authority whether that default might be broadened from affordable housing to allow occupation also by those whose jobs might be seen as critical to the life of rural communities, such as policemen, doctors, teachers, community nurses or clergy, who might not necessarily qualify under the provisions for affordable housing. That might be particularly appropriate in areas with poor access to public transport, potentially less suitable for affordable housing but where such posts are nonetheless important.

4.7   Exemption from Enforcement Action

4.7.1   Breach of a condition on occupation will be a change of use for development control purposes and if done without permission can lead to the LPA taking enforcement action. However, where such a breach endures for ten years, it becomes statutorily immune from enforcement (s.171B, TCPA 1990 for England and Wales; s.124(3) of the 1997 Act for Scotland).

4.7.2   Following some widely reported cases over the concealed construction of dwellings, s.124 of the Localism Act 2011 introduced new sections 171BA to 171BC into the 1990 Act for England and Wales to provide further enforcement powers where an apparent breach of planning control has been "deliberately concealed". While there appear to be no cases on this, it seems likely that simple inaction over a breach of an occupancy condition is not "deliberate" concealment though dishonest replies to inquiries would perhaps be such.

4.7.3   Thus, if an applicant can demonstrate that a property has been occupied in breach of an agricultural occupancy condition for more than ten years, then an application can be made to the LPA for a Certificate of Lawfulness of Existing Use or Development (CLEUD) under s.191 TCPA 1990. The equivalent Scottish provisions for a Certificate of Lawful Use or Development are at s.150 of the 1997 Act.

4.7.4   This is a matter of fact, rather than policy, so provided that the applicant can produce sufficient evidence of the breach, then the local authority should award a CLEUD.

4.7.5   It has to be stressed that the evidence must show that the breach was continuous for the ten year period and so any break in occupation should not be significant. For example, if the property was empty for a few weeks between tenants in order to allow time for re-decoration, that might not be considered a significant break, but if the property was empty for several months between tenants because it was difficult to re-let, that could be sufficient for there to be a break of the occupation in breach. With no hard and fast rules, each case must be argued on its merits.

4.7.6   Detailed records of who occupied the property, what their occupation was and how long they were in occupation will be needed. Thus, showing that it had been let out to a series of teachers for more than ten years would support an application but discovering that in between such lets it had been occupied, even briefly, by someone working on a nearby farm (or retired from such work) could be fatal to it.

4.7.7   It is suggested that the evidence should be marshalled, tested and then an appropriate statutory declaration drafted and declared to cover it. It may also be prudent for witnesses, such as previous occupiers of the dwelling, to attest by statutory declaration.

4.7.8   The effect of a CLEUD is that the occupation of the property in breach of the condition is not unlawful. It does not remove the condition altogether and there is a risk that an occupier who complied with the condition could render the Certificate invalid, in which case the ten year time period for establishing non-compliance would start again.

4.7.9   An application for a CLEUD might also be appropriate where the planning permission was not implemented exactly in accordance with the consent as, for example, where a planning consent was given to build a house subject to an agricultural occupancy condition. If the house was constructed in a different location from that specified in the planning consent then the house as constructed would not have planning permission. If it was then lived in as a single dwelling for four years without enforcement action being taken, the owner could apply for a CLEUD – four years being the relevant period for both operational works and use as a single dwelling (subject to cases over concealment). The Certificate would then be unconstrained by any limitation on occupancy because the planning consent to which the condition attached was not implemented.

4.7.10   Careful consideration should be given and, as necessary specialist advice taken, on such non-standard matters so that they are properly understood. For example, a failure to discharge all the conditions for a development may mean that it is in breach anyway.

4.8   Lifting a Restriction Imposed by Planning Agreement or Obligation

4.8.1   Sometimes an occupancy restriction may not be imposed by a condition but through a planning agreement under what is now s.106 of the Town and Country Planning Act 1990 (previously s.52) – s.75 of the Scottish 1997 Act; Article 40, Planning (Northern Ireland) Order 1991. This regime is discussed at 3.8 above. Commitments under it can only lifted by mutual agreement with LPA or by the formal procedures for it to be modified or discharged.

4.8.2   In England and Wales, planning agreements made before the changes to s.106 made by the Planning and Compensation Act 1991 were treated as restrictive covenants with recourse under s.84 of the Law of Property Act 1925 to the Upper Tribunal (Lands Chamber) – formerly the Lands Tribunal. This is a separate legal regime:

> "Nobody was obliged to enter into a section [52] agreement. If an appellant for planning permission was offered permission upon terms that he entered into a section [52] agreement he could appeal to the Secretary of State. But if he chose to enter into the agreement he (and his successors in title) must accept that he can only avoid its effect through the statutory procedure under section 84. But it seems to me that while the two regimes impinge upon each other to some extent, they constitute different systems of control and each has, and retains, an independent existence." (*Re Martins' Application*)

For an example of this see the *Rasbridge* case below.

4.8.3   Since the 1991 changes, a party bound by an obligation can also apply to the LPA for its modification or discharge with a right of appeal to the Secretary of State (ss.106A and 106B, TCPA). However, this opportunity only becomes available five years after the obligation was made. S.84 of the Law of Property Act is not available for planning obligations.

4.8.4   In Scotland, an appeal against a refusal to remove or modify an obligation or agreement can be made to Scottish ministers (the Directorate for Planning and Environmental Appeals). The Scottish Government's Chief Planner, recognising some dispute, wrote to Heads of Planning in July 2011 to confirm that the new procedures for such applications applied to all agreements and obligations under s.75, whatever their date.

4.8.5   The approach to a pre-1991 s.106 agreement has recently been tested in the Welsh case, *Rasbridge*. Here, the Upper Tribunal (Lands Chamber) refused an application to lift an agricultural occupancy restriction as obsolete because the applicants had failed to demonstrate that the market had been properly tested. The bungalow had been built in 1986 on a 156 acre farm near Swansea with consent subject to an agreement under s.52 of TCPA 1971 restricting occupation to those:
> "... solely or mainly employed or last employed in the locality in agriculture ...".
Since then, several barns on the farm had been converted into a further four dwellings and the bungalow itself was extended substantially in 2002, all with full planning consent. Applications to lift the agricultural tie on the bungalow, on the ground that it was no longer needed for such a use, had been refused by the local authority in 2007 and again in 2009. An appeal against the second refusal brought the applicants to the Upper Tribunal.

4.8.6   The test of whether a restriction is obsolete is whether the restriction is still capable of fulfilling its original purpose (*Re Truman, Hanbury, Buxton and Co Ltd's Application*) and its purpose was seen to be that expressed in the condition.

4.8.7   The Tribunal referred to relevant planning policies. The adopted local plan stated that removal of an agricultural occupancy restriction will only be permitted where:
> "... it can be demonstrated that the agricultural need advanced at the time of the original permission no longer applies and there is no need for the dwelling to meet the long term needs of the local agricultural community or those employed in associated agricultural services. Evidence will be required of the property having been offered for sale and to rent with the occupancy condition at a realistic 'affordable' price to the agricultural community and associated agricultural services, over an acceptable period of appropriately targeted marketing."

4.8.8   Welsh policy was set out in TAN 6: Planning for Sustainable Rural Communities. The applicants were not seeking to have the agreement modified to reflect rural enterprise dwelling policy.

4.8.9   The Tribunal noted (apparently pointedly) that:
> "Both parties rely upon market testing as the best indicator of whether the restriction is capable of fulfilling a demonstrable need to house agricultural workers."
That leaves it an open question as to the outcome of the case had that premise not been accepted by the parties since the decision is solely concerned with this basis for assessing the obsolescence of the condition.

4.8.10   The TAN 6 Practice Guidance states that:
> "The long-standing mechanism for demonstrating the absence of need has been market testing."

That market testing should continue for a "reasonable period" of at least 12 months and be carried out in such a way so that:

- the availability of a property is advertised in such a manner that compliant purchasers or tenants are likely to be made aware of it; and
- the price or rent attached to a property reflects the restrictive occupancy requirement.

4.8.11   The applicants marketed the bungalow for sale through a local firm of agents between June 2008 and September 2009. It had been advertised repeatedly in the local press and on four internet sites. The unencumbered value of the property was estimated at £450,000 and it was initially offered at £325,000 – a 28% discount. The price was dropped twice during the marketing period so that a discount of 39% eventually applied, but despite a number of telephone enquiries, there were no applications to view the property and no offers to purchase it.

4.8.12   The Tribunal did not accept arguments put by the Local Authority that:

- more land should have been made available with the bungalow (it was offered with 0.5 acres)
- the agents should have recorded the details of all those who enquired about it, regardless of whether or not they took their enquiry any further.

However, it accepted the arguments that the marketing exercise had not been sufficiently rigorous to demonstrate that there was no demand for the property (the case had been fought on that basis) subject to the occupancy condition:

- the property had not been marketed for rent: planning policy required the market for both sale and rent to be tested.
- the applicants' agents had not analysed their comparable evidence objectively.
- the marketing exercise should have included advertisements in the national farming press.
- the adjustments in the asking price over the marketing period had not reflected the variations in the general property market and could not be distinguished from the discount attributable to the planning condition.

The decision illustrates the need to check local and national planning policy carefully before embarking on a marketing exercise, to ensure that it can be seen to meet the relevant tests – here there was an obligation to offer for rent.

4.8.13   The same concerns apply to marketing exercises for planning agreements as for conditions (see 4.3.8). They may be appropriate where the owner is prepared to sell or let the property to a qualifying occupier (as was the case in *Rasbridge*) but not where there is no intention to conclude such a transaction.

5. PLANNING POLICY IN ENGLAND FOR RURAL WORKERS' DWELLINGS

5.1 General

5.1.1 In England, the Localism Act 2011 is a key piece of legislation applying several parts of the present Government's policy (with the potential tensions between them):

- a reduction in central government regulation
- a desire to see planning policy enable or stimulate economic activity (the Act was introduced at a time when there were few signs of recovery in the economy)
- the developing emphasis on "sustainability"
- the view that LPAs, accountable to their electorates, should generally take responsibility for setting their own development control policies, having regard to the new National Planning Policy Framework (NPPF).

5.1.2 The NPPF was then produced in March 2012, setting out basic approaches to policies in an environment in which many planning authorities have adopted plans but many have not. As will be seen in the context of rural workers' dwellings, much existing guidance was simultaneously withdrawn. That has led to some uncertainty surrounding local plan documents in some local authority areas. Where the local authority is still moving into the new regime, the weight attached to policies may change over time. **Agricultural valuers engaging in planning work should ensure that they are familiar with the current content of relevant local plan documents**. They may also find it helpful to engage with the forward policy teams of relevant local authorities in order to understand the material weight which can be attached to any particular policy.

5.1.3 Many LPAs do not as yet have approved plans while a growing number do. Where approved plans are in place they may take a range of approaches to the exceptions for development outside settlements:

- some written before the NPPF was in place may have implicitly relied on PPS7 Annex A and so say little about the subject
- others, again usually those written before the NPPF, will have expressly incorporated or followed Annex A.
- yet more, often later plans, will follow the wider approach of the NPPF or have drafted their own policy.

There will be plans that do not carry full weight because of deficiencies in procedure and some Councils with plans will also use unadopted ancillary guidance. The simple fact that a Council is relying on a document does not give it authority.

5.1.4 In the absence of an approved local plan, the effective planning policy regime is the NPPF with its central presumption in favour of sustainable development.

5.1.5 It becomes more complex where there are local plans. The NPPF provides that existing local plans:

"should not be considered out-of-date simply because they were adopted prior to the publication of this Framework" (para 211).

"However, the policies contained in this Framework are material considerations which local planning authorities should take into account from the day of its publication." (para 212)

"… due weight should be given to relevant policies in existing plans according to their degree of consistency with this framework (the closer the policies in the plan to the policies in the Framework, the greater the weight that may be given)." (para 215).

5.1.6   Older plans may therefore have less weight on points where they are in conflict with the NPPF.

5.1.7   As the NPPF "aims to strengthen local decision making and reinforce the importance of up-to-date plans" (para 209) its paragraph 213 prompts full or partial reviews of plans to take its policies into account. As part of that:
> "decision-takers may also give weight to relevant policies in emerging plans according to:
>   • the stage of preparation of the emerging plan (the more advanced the preparation, the greater the weight that may be given);
>   • the extent to which there are unresolved objections to relevant policies (the less significant the unresolved objections, the greater the weight that may be given); and
>   • the degree of consistency of the relevant policies in the emerging plan to the policies in this Framework (the closer the policies in the emerging plan to the policies in the Framework, the greater the weight that may be given)."

5.1.8   Thus, it could be that where a provision in an older plan is in conflict with the NPPF it might, according to the circumstances, be given lesser weight in determining an application.

5.1.9   The resulting position was described in *Scrivens* by the High Court:
> "The NPPF is not a plan nor is it to be regarded as a policy statement within the meaning of Part 2 of the Planning Act 2008 – see s.5 of that Act. It is however a material consideration"

5.1.10   Even with a development plan:
> "… section 38(6) leaves to decision-maker [the LPA] the assessment of the facts and the weighting of the considerations material to the decision … It is for the decision-maker to assess the relative weight to be given to all material considerations, including the policies of the development plan. Whether there are considerations of sufficient weight to indicate that the development plan should not be accorded the priority given to it by statute is a question for the decision-maker, not the court." (*Thakeham Village Action v Horsham District Council* referring to the House of Lords decision in *Edinburgh City Council v Secretary of State for Scotland*)

5.1.11 The Place of Supporting Documents – Local authorities may not only have adopted plans with policies but also supporting documents. The status of these has been considered in *Cherkley v Mole Valley* where the Secretary of State had saved a pre-2004 policy relevant to golf courses and the place of supporting text was at issue in applying it. The Court of Appeal, reversing a High Court decision, advised that:
> "The supporting text consists of *descriptive and explanatory matter* in respect of the policies and/or a *reasoned justification* of the policies. That text is plainly relevant to the interpretation of a policy to which it relates but it is not itself a policy or part of a policy, it does not have the force of policy and it cannot trump the policy. I do not think that a development that accorded with the policies in the local plan could be said not to conform with the plan because it failed to satisfy an additional criterion referred to only in the supporting text. That applies even where, as here, the local plan states that the supporting text indicates how the policies will be implemented."

The supporting text suggested that "need" should be shown but this was not among the criteria set by the policy itself. This was more than descriptive, explanatory or justifying text. It could not be relied on to bring the additional factor of "need" into the policy which did not include it.

5.2 Examples of Local Plan Policies for Rural Workers' Dwellings

5.2.1 At the time of writing (October 2014), examples include:

- Bromsgrove District Council's Supplementary Planning Guidance Note 6, dealing with agricultural dwellings and occupancy conditions, was adopted in January 2004, long before the NPPF was even thought of, and largely reproduces Annex A of PPS7.

- North York Moors National Park Core Strategy and Development Policies of 2008 again naturally followed Annex A. In December 2012, it published Planning Advice Note 6: Agricultural and Other Essential Rural Workers' Dwellings again reproducing much of the wording of Annex A and indicating that applications for both agricultural and other rural workers' dwellings will be assessed against those criteria. That document is not a Supplementary Planning Document or a Development Plan Document but the Park argues that "the principles it contains were accepted as part of the adoption of the Core Strategy through reference to Annex A of former PPS7 in paragraph 9.14 of the Core Strategy".

- New Forest District Council which adopted its Local Plan Part 2 in April 2014 using very similar wording to PPS7 Annex A for its policy on new permanent dwellings for agricultural or forestry workers outside of the National Park boundary.

- Cotswold District Council which sought to bring in PPS7 Annex A as supplementary planning guidance but as it failed to consult properly on the process the document cannot be given full weight.

- Amber Valley has a broader rural housing policy H5 offering a third exception for dwellings outside settlements for "new development which can be shown to be necessary for the operation of a rural based activity and where countryside location is essential".

5.2.2 Upper Eden Neighbourhood Development Plan 2012-2025 provides both a rural exception policy UENDP1 for single plots for affordable housing meeting a local need, supported by a s.106 agreement and a policy for housing for farms and rural businesses:

"UENDP2 Housing on Farms

"Established farm enterprises or rural businesses may have additional dwellings that can be used by family members, holiday letting or renting to local people. Applications for any additional housing must be accompanied by justification for at least one of the forms of housing that the policy intends to permit. In addition it will be subject to a Section 106 Legal Agreement which specifically permits the use of the property to housing for family members, holiday letting, farm worker, and for rent to local people. The Section 106 Agreement will prevent the sale of the property except as part of the farm enterprise or rural business or alternatively, as an affordable dwelling.

"In the case of tenant farmers who need to manage a generational transition and build a property which they will own, the new dwelling need not be tied to the main farm holding. It will be secured by a s.106 agreement to be used only for agricultural workers, holiday letting, or local occupancy or affordable housing.

"Consideration of the siting and design of such new houses will be important to allow both the flexibility that the policy intends and also ensuring that there will be no unacceptable impact upon the visual or landscape amenity of the area. The reuse of an existing traditional building within the landscape or a suitable plot within or near to the existing farmyard, may prove to be a suitable site."

5.3 National Planning Policy Guidance

5.3.1 Background – With the basic administrative needs of such a planning system and the many and varying policy objectives, the government has long issued guidance on operation of necessarily very broad planning policies. These have variously been through:

- Circulars – such as the last major liberalisation of the planning system under Circular 22/80
- White Papers
- Planning Policy Guidance notes (PPGs), Minerals Planning Guidance notes and Regional Planning Guidance
- Planning Policy Statements (PPSs).

5.3.2 Guidance Now Withdrawn – All Planning Policy Statements and much other guidance were withdrawn on the introduction of the NPPF in March 2012. Annex 3 of the NPPF lists the documents replaced by the Framework (see Appendix 2 to this paper).

5.3.3 The Planning Policy Guidance notes covered general policy (PPG1) and various topics such as the green belt (PPG2), land for housing (PPG3) and development in the countryside (PPG7). It was PPG7 that set out, among other issues, guidance as to policy on agricultural workers' dwellings (see its Annexe A). PPGs were gradually replaced by Planning Policy Statements (PPSs) and PPS7 (Sustainable Development in Rural Areas) applied for rural development control. Its relevant statements on agricultural workers' dwellings are set out at Appendix 1 to this paper.

5.3.4 PPS7 has been withdrawn in that process and so its detailed guidance on agricultural workers' dwellings has ceased to have any official force. As it is both relevant to the historic development of the present positon and some approved plans expressly invoke or draw on it, its Annexe A is set out at Appendix 1.

5.3.5 Thus, unless a local planning authority had expressly included Annex A or any similar wording into its approved local plan, the statements in the NPPF reviewed next are now the relevant policy regime for rural housing. **In such cases, LPAs, applicants and others should not now look to PPS7 for any authoritative guidance**, albeit that, as the product of evolution, it may still represent thoughts and approaches that may be relevant and reviewed so long as they are consistent with the NPPF – that issue is considered below.

5.4 The National Planning Policy Framework

5.4.1 The National Planning Policy Framework (NPPF) was published on 27th March 2012. At the time of writing, it can be downloaded from the Planning Portal website.

5.4.2 The NPPF sets out the Government's general policies for development control. Ministers were clear that they wished to replace over 1,000 pages of guidance with some 50 pages of principles, within which there was to be more discretion. National policy was looking for that discretion to be used positively, especially with widely reported concerns that the planning system was frustrating economic recovery and progress.

5.4.3   The NPPF is to be taken into account when considering planning applications and appeals and when preparing development plans.

5.4.4   Sustainable Development – Its key statement on this is the central presumption in favour of sustainable development encompassing economic, environmental and social sustainability. Paragraph 14 of the NPPF states that the presumption:
> "should be seen as a golden thread running through both plan-making and decision-taking".

5.4.5   General Rural Policy – That commitment to sustainable growth in terms of the rural economy is dealt with at paragraph 28 of the NPPF:
> "Planning policies should support economic growth in rural areas in order to create jobs and prosperity by taking a positive approach to sustainable new development. To promote a strong rural economy, local and neighbourhood plans should:
> - support the sustainable growth and expansion of all types of business and enterprise in rural areas, both through conversion of existing buildings and well designed new buildings;
> - promote the development and diversification of agricultural and other land-based rural businesses;
> - support sustainable rural tourism and leisure developments that benefit businesses in rural areas, communities and visitors, and which respect the character of the countryside. This should include supporting the provision and expansion of tourist and visitor facilities in appropriate locations where identified needs are not met by existing facilities in rural service centres; and
> - promote the retention and development of local services and community facilities in villages, such as local shops, meeting places, sports venues, cultural buildings, public houses and places of worship."

5.4.6   Nothing in that casts any direct light on the official approach to rural workers' housing but it sets a focus on business and economic growth.

5.4.7   Rural Housing Policy – The general approach to rural housing is set out at paragraph 55 of the NPPF which opens:
> "To promote sustainable development in rural areas, housing should be located where it will enhance or maintain the vitality of rural communities. For example, where there are groups of smaller settlements, development in one village may support services in a village nearby. Local planning authorities should avoid new isolated homes in the countryside."

5.4.8   Those opening sentences set out the longstanding policy view. However, four exceptions are then provided to that general policy, the first for rural workers' dwellings and others which may also be relevant on occasion. The paragraph continues to read:
> "…unless there are special circumstances such as:
> - the essential need for a rural worker to live permanently at or near their place of work in the countryside; or
> - where such development would represent the optimal viable use of a heritage asset or would be appropriate enabling development to secure the future of heritage assets; or
> - where the development would re-use redundant or disused buildings and lead to an enhancement to the immediate setting; or
> - the exceptional quality or innovative nature of the design of the dwelling. Such a design should:

- be truly outstanding or innovative, helping to raise standards of design more generally in rural areas;
- reflect the highest standards in architecture;
- significantly enhance its immediate setting; and
- be sensitive to the defining characteristics of the local area."

5.4.9   These exceptions cover previous policy areas but not necessarily in the same terms – most notably for rural workers' housing considered further below:
  – Bullet 2 is the policy basis for promoting housing either as:
    - an "optimal viable use" of "heritage assets". A heritage asset is a broadly defined in the NPPF as one which has "a degree of significance meriting consideration in planning decisions, because of its heritage interest". It goes beyond listed buildings to include monuments, sites and places, and it specifically includes local listing.
    - a source of funds to secure the future of such assets ("enabling development")
  – Bullet 3 is positive policy on the re-use of either redundant or dis-used buildings (agricultural or otherwise) as housing.
  – Bullet 4 carries forward the exception introduced by John Gummer, when the relevant Minister, for new country houses.
It will be important for those involved with rural housing applications to understand these exceptions.

5.4.10   However, having put the NPPF in place, the policy cycle has turned and the Government has begun to publish revised and updated guidance on its Planning Portal website from March 2014. The guidance covers
- procedural issues, such as "Making an Application"
- general subjects, such as "Design"
- technical subjects, such as "Rural Housing".

5.4.11 Rural Housing Guidance – This statement of Guidance issued in March 2014 simply states:
"How should local authorities support sustainable rural communities?
- It is important to recognise the particular issues facing rural areas in terms of housing supply and affordability, and the role of housing in supporting the broader sustainability of villages and smaller settlements. This is clearly set out in the National Planning Policy Framework, in the core planning principles, the section on supporting a prosperous rural economy and the section on housing.
- A thriving rural community in a living, working countryside depends, in part, on retaining local services and community facilities such as schools, local shops, cultural venues, public houses and places of worship. Rural housing is essential to ensure viable use of these local facilities.
- Assessing housing need and allocating sites should be considered at a strategic level and through the Local Plan and/or neighbourhood plan process. However, all settlements can play a role in delivering sustainable development in rural areas – and so blanket policies restricting housing development in some settlements and preventing other settlements from expanding should be avoided unless their use can be supported by robust evidence.
- The National Planning Policy Framework also recognises that different sustainable transport policies and measures will be required in different communities and opportunities to maximise sustainable transport solutions will vary from urban to rural areas."

5.4.12 While again broadly supportive of development in rural communities, this guidance is at the level of general principle and does not add anything direct to the NPPF's policy for rural workers' housing.

5.5 Applying the NPPF to Rural Workers' Housing Within Settlements

Applications for dwellings within identified settlements will turn on the ordinary policies for housing. It may be that the exemptions for dwellings on isolated sites would be seen to be relevant for settlements for which an approved plan does not provide for development.

5.6 Applying the NPPF to Housing Outside Settlements

5.6.1 Where there is a relevant approved local plan that will, in principle, govern local development policy including that for rural workers' housing, subject to the circumstances of the case in hand. That plan itself should be consistent with the NPPF.

5.6.2 However, at the time of writing there will be many LPAs that do not have relevant approved plans. Applications for rural housing are then to be handled under the policies of the NPPF.

5.6.3 An Initial Approach – Within the general principle of sustainable development, that process could proceed along the following lines:

- **Is the proposal for an "isolated home"?** If not, it falls under the general opening statement of NPPF paragraph 55 and the March 2014 Rural Housing Guidance
- Can it be justified under one or more of the other three exceptions from the presumptions against "isolated homes"?
  - **Can a "heritage asset" be re-used to provide the accommodation?** Would that be the optimal viable use of the asset? The alternative option for "enabling development" seems likely to be less relevant as that may generally see the new housing sold rather than retained.
  - **Is there a redundant or dis-used building available whose use as a home would enhance the immediate setting?** This is entirely independent of the new permitted development use class for English agricultural buildings to be re-used as dwellings (see Chapter 6). This exception applies equally to buildings that are "redundant" and to those that are dis-used although there are no further definitions in the NPPF.
  - **Could it be within the exceptional design exception?** Originally seen as an exception for new country mansions, nothing in the wording used here necessarily appears to require such scale though the building "should … significantly enhance its immediate setting". That might cover a farmhouse and, perhaps in certain circumstances, a cottage. However the requirements of this exception are likely to make this an expensive option.

5.6.4 The Rural Workers' Housing Exception – The NPPF's wording for this is new and so untested by the courts (save for *Embleton* – see 5.6.6-7 below). The analysis here offers an initial exploration of the wording which reads:

"Local planning authorities should avoid new isolated homes in the countryside unless there are special circumstances such as:
- the essential need for a rural worker to live permanently at or near their place of work in the countryside;".

This now countenances occupation by a wider group of people than the previous policy for agricultural and forestry workers.

5.6.5   Key points in this appear to be that:
- the exception applies to proposals for an "isolated home"
- it is predicated on there being "**a place of work in the countryside**". That is not necessarily a business, but rather a place of employment. It has to be in the countryside but with no other test – it just has to exist. There is no equivalent to the three year viability test of the old PPS7. If an LPA sensed that the place of work was not viable it might question whether the exemption applied.
- is a "**rural worker**" needed for it? It is not clear what is added by the adjective "rural" at this point. It could be circular and add nothing. A stronger interpretation could be that not only does the place of work have to be in the countryside, but the work should in some way be "rural". The easier reading, that it defines the worker, seems hardest to apply within the development control regime. In any event, this is no longer limited to workers in agriculture or forestry. This is discussed further below at 5.6.8.
- is there an **essential need for that worker to live at or near the place of work**? That could appear close to the functional test of the former PPS7 but now to be applied in the context of any work in the countryside. While "need" is often used in a general way, it is qualified by "essential" and so may mean something more than "helpful". Presumably, the need is driven by the work concerned. This is perhaps the part of the exception that may be most clearly tested and so is considered further below. The Court of Appeal considered the approach to "need" in *Cherkley*, commenting that

    "The word "need" has a protean or chameleon-like character ... and is capable of encompassing necessity at one end of the spectrum and demand or desire at the other. The particular meaning to be attached to it ... depends on context. ... [In the specific golf course case] "need" is to be understood in a broad sense so that the requirement is capable of being met by establishing the existence of a demand for the proposed type of facility which is not being met by existing facilities."

- is that a **permanent need**? This is taken to exclude temporary needs but to leave it open to question whether regular extended seasonal needs (as for fruit or block calving) qualify or not.

5.6.6   In *Embleton,* the Court noted agreement by the parties that "the guidance in paragraph 55 of NPPF is significantly less onerous than in PPS 7".

5.6.7   It is particularly noted that this policy does not repeat the financial test of PPS 7. That has now been considered in *Embleton*, the one case so far with any significant review of the NPPF's rural worker exception, which affirmed that the NPPF indeed sets **no** financial test by which to judge applications. The judge said:

    "... I accept that the test under paragraph 55 of NPPF is different from the test under Annex A, paragraph 12(iii) of PPS7. In particular, I do not accept ... that the NPPF requires that the proposal is economically viable. ... The NPPF test simply requires a judgment of whether the proposed agricultural enterprise has an essential need for a worker to be there or near there."

5.6.8   Rural Worker – This exception to general policy now has a wider application to "rural workers" rather than just agriculture and forestry, allowing those employed in other sectors to demonstrate an essential need for accommodation. As with all other features of the principles-based approach of the NPPF, there are no definitions and so an understanding of the limits of this phrase will have to be developed in practice.

5.6.9   A point that appears significant is that the worker must have a place of work – that need not be a business. It is perhaps therefore the employer's needs that seem to drive the assessment. That suggests that this could include, for example:
 – a gamekeeper
 – a groom employed to look after horses kept for recreational purposes
 – a warden employed to manage a wildlife reserve
 – a housekeeper
provided that the "essential need" test was met.

5.6.10   It seems reasonable to assume that all those currently accepted as qualifying agricultural and forestry workers would ordinarily be accepted as rural workers.

5.6.11   The review of what may count as "rural enterprises" in the Welsh TAN 6 Practice Guidance Paper of December 2011 may offer some illumination even if some points may appear open to argument:
 "This extension applies primarily to land-related businesses which, directly or indirectly, need to be located in the countryside rather than in existing settlements." (Para 1.7)
Alongside agriculture and forestry, this can include:
 – "the exploitation of mineral and water resources and other forms of land management" (Para 2.4)
 – "substantive equine and fishery enterprises, kennels, catteries and veterinary facilities" (Para 2.5).
 – businesses with a strong degree of interaction of on-site processing of primary production with the land management (as with making cheese on a dairy farm) (Para 2.6)
 – practical services such as relief labour, land management contracting (silaging, fencing, walling), veterinary or farriery services but probably not general services to land management (such as building maintenance or professional services such as accountancy or agronomy) (Para 2.7)
 – key elements of the workforce for tourism, leisure and conservation that need to be appropriately housed close to their work in the countryside (Para 2.8).

5.6.12   There is no requirement in the NPPF that the worker be full time; the policy concern is that the worker is needed to be close to the rural place of employment.

5.6.13   In addition to decisions directly for planning, case law has sought to define who counts as an agricultural worker for the purposes of other legislation.

5.6.14   In considering the protection of the Rent (Agriculture) Act 1976, the Court of Appeal in *McPhail v Greensmith* found that a mechanic employed on the farm was working in agriculture just as much as his co-workers who drove the tractors. However, *Earl of Normanton v Giles* found that a gamekeeper was not an agricultural worker. It seems likely that both of those examples could fall within the description of a "rural worker" for the purposes of the NPPF.

5.6.15   The IHT case, *Atkinson*, considered the occupation of a cottage for the purpose of agriculture. In exploring what this might mean, the Upper Tribunal allowed that a bookkeeper fully occupied on the farm could qualify for that – though as the Practice Guide to TAN 6 suggests it might be harder to show the essential need for a bookkeeper living so close to work (see 7.5.12 below).

5.6.16 Essential Need – The NPPF requires demonstration that there is "the essential need for a rural worker to live permanently at or near their place of work". It is not clear if the use of "essential" adds anything to a strict sense of the meaning of "need".

5.6.17 The obvious parallel is with the functional tests for PPS7 Annexe A (see Appendix 1 for the full text) which required the applicant to demonstrate that it was essential for the proper functioning of the enterprise that a worker was readily available at most times. Annexe A offered to two illustrations for this in its agricultural context:

a) *In case animals or agricultural processes require essential care at short notice.*
This might include:
- Animal health and welfare, such as the care of very young animals, the supervision of sick animals or management of animals which were due to give birth.
- Monitoring environmental conditions in intensive livestock units and being on hand to deal with emergencies.

b) *To deal quickly with emergencies that could otherwise cause serious loss of crops or products, for example, by frost damage or the failure of automatic systems.*
This could include:
- Management of environmental control systems in glasshouses and mushroom sheds, where this cannot be done remotely or where emergency back-up may be required.
- Frost mitigation for tender plants or nursery stock.

5.6.18 This was sometimes referred to as the "sight and sound test" in emphasising the perceived need for accommodation directly on site.

5.6.19 That policy did not recognise the desire for someone to live on site for security reasons as an adequate ground. That may now be more available under the NPPF subject to proof of circumstances, particularly if evidence of past incidents of theft or vandalism can be produced. A business that is refused insurance cover because it does not have someone living on site may have a case.

5.6.20 Bearing in mind that this could be tested for any worker needed by a place of work in the countryside, it may be that tests might be met by:
- any 24 hour process needing supervision, whether an AD plant or robotic milking as much as the examples given above
- a 24 hour need for personal care
- a location to which travel is vulnerable to disruption by, say, snow or because it is an island.

While the previous functional test may still cast some light on this new broader policy, it seems clear that the previous financial test offers little to analysis of the NPPF policy here.

5.6.21 The Welsh Practice Guidance to TAN 6 also considers examples of uses where there is an essential need to be resident by the business which may aid thinking and discussion of the same question in England. Its paragraph 4.5 says:

"Functional need is primarily concerned with the management of risk within the operations of an enterprise such that, without the ready attention of a worker(s), any particular event or combination of events could lead to adverse animal welfare, crop or product quality, or health and safety consequences which might threaten the stability and economic well-being of an enterprise. In all cases, these would be circumstances which could not be properly managed within normal working hours."

5.6.22　That is then developed by 4.6 with examples such as:
- where immediate, regular and often unpredictable care over much of the year is required to safeguard the specific welfare of livestock and offspring in breeding programmes, for example in lambing, calving and foaling conditions.
- where the more general welfare of animals housed in buildings either permanently or for protracted periods, for example in intensive livestock units, stud and livery stables, or commercial kennels.
- where the productive processes or the quality of crops and products are dependent upon the maintenance and security of controlled environments using automated systems, such as in protected cropping horticulture and intensive livestock units. However, it is often possible to achieve adequate surveillance through remote means such as CCTV and temperature and other environmental sensors.
- where the delivery of specialist services is required outside normal hours and where timeliness of response is important.
- where the lack of 24-hour on-site supervision may prejudice the commercial viability of a business, for example at a large established livery yard.

5.6.23　Permission for Temporary Accommodation? – The NPPF is drafted in terms of permanent needs and appears to imply permanent dwellings. Recurrent extended seasonal uses (such as for fruit or block calving) have been discussed above but there appears to be a gap for temporary uses. In practice, LPAs have used temporary permissions (and so usually for caravans/mobile homes) to give an applicant a chance to prove his case.

5.6.24　In some areas, the matter may anyway be covered by adopted plans but it seems probable that, as a matter of practice, such an approach will continue and could also offer a means to handle more transient but necessary cases – indeed, *Embleton* concerned a three year permission for a temporary caravan.

5.6.25　If the temporary accommodation would be a caravan, there may be an interaction with the site licensing provisions of the Caravan Sites and Control of Development Act 1960 for England, Wales and Scotland. A caravan here is
"any structure designed or adapted for human habitation which is capable of being moved from one place to another (whether by being towed, or by being transported on a motor vehicle or trailer) and any motor vehicle so designed or adapted, but does not include … any tent" (s.29).
The Act's Schedule 1 provides a number of exemptions from the need for a licence. These include the accommodation on agricultural land "during a particular season of a person or persons employed in farming operations on land in the same occupation" with a similar provision for seasonal use by forestry workers.

5.6.26　Alternative Accommodation? – *Embleton* considered whether it was irrational (a test for judicial review) for a LPA to accept that the essential need could not be met by taking a nearby shorthold tenancy that was available:
"It was a matter for their judgment whether such a need could be satisfied by a short let of No.3. A short term let is terminable after 6 months which is far shorter than the three years for which the temporary permission is granted. In those circumstances the decision to grant the permission cannot in my view be said to be irrational or unreasonable."

5.6.27   In *Keen v Secretary of State for the Environment*, a 1996 case, concerning a part-time farmer wanting to retire and take on a full time stockman while staying on in his farmhouse, the Inspector had turned the appeal down as he thought that the farmer could make part of his house available to the man and his wife. The judge demurred:

> "Having established the need, it is reasonable to expect clear-cut planning reasons as to why it should not be met in the way proposed unless other available and suitable accommodation exists. ... Accommodation may *de facto* exist but its availability and suitability must be subjected to some scrutiny ... Nor is there any material or any sufficient material to justify a conclusion, which *prima facie* flies in the face of good sense, that a house of this kind is suitable."

5.6.28   That view was endorsed in 2008 on not dissimilar facts in *JR Cussons and Son v Secretary of State for Communities and Local Government*. If sharing the farmhouse was argued as a viable alternative, then:

> "there was a need to explore the practicalities of that suggestion in greater detail".

5.6.29   Occupancy Conditions – While these are discussed further below, it seems likely that permissions for rural workers' dwellings will be subject to occupancy conditions. As with the present agricultural occupancy condition, the drafting of those conditions will need to consider a number of points, which may include:

– the position of others living with the worker, family or otherwise, whether or not dependent on the worker
– the position of the worker when retired, out of work or in a new job elsewhere
– the classes of workers who may occupy the property
– the position of the worker's widow/er or other members of the household after the worker's death or removal.

5.6.30   Naturally, there is no model for a Rural Workers' Housing condition in the surviving Appendix A to Circular 11/95. The rural enterprise occupancy condition offered in the Welsh TAN 6 (see 7.6.9) may offer a model for adaptation, though the English policy does not provide the fallback to use for affordable housing when the dwelling is not needed for a rural enterprise worker.

5.6.31   So far as the early experience of appeal decisions since the introduction of the NPPF is helpful, it may indicate that Inspectors have tended to approve occupancy conditions that are relatively tightly drawn to the business of the appellant, rather than applying more general rural workers' conditions, whether:

– limiting occupation of the dwelling to the particular business (using the same approach as the standard agriculture condition. For example,

> "Occupation of the dwelling house hereby permitted shall be limited to a worker solely or primarily employed in the management of the kennels, cattery, and equestrian centre known as Willows Wags and Whiskers, Willows Stables, Goodshaw Lane, Rossendale, Lancashire BB4 8TN and their partner and resident dependants." (APP/B2355/A/12/2184388)

or
– by adding the specific business to agriculture and forestry in the standard condition as in a 2013 definition. For example,

> "The occupation of the dwelling shall be limited to a person solely or mainly working, or last working in the locality in either agriculture, forestry, or in the commercial breeding of horses, or a widow or widower of such a person, and to any resident dependants." (APP/H0738/A/13/2193698)

However, such cases do not mean that a broader "rural worker" approach will not develop.

6. PERMITTED DEVELOPMENT IN ENGLAND: CONVERSION OF AGRICULTURAL BUILDINGS TO DWELLINGS

6.1 New Opportunities for Agricultural Buildings in England: Use Classes M and MA

6.1.1   There have been a number of recent extensions to the General Permitted Development Order of 1995 to allow the conversion of agricultural buildings to other uses. These are only available in England. With the qualified rights to convert agricultural buildings to dwellings under Class MB reviewed in section 6.2, this section briefly reviews other recently created conversion rights

6.1.2   **Commercial Uses** – A new Use Class M allows conditional rights for the conversion of a building and land within its curtilage from use as an agricultural building (turning on its use as at 3rd July 2012) to a range of commercial uses, namely:
- shops (Class A1)
- financial and professional services (Class A2)
- restaurants and cafes (Class A3)
- business (light industrial/office – Class B1)
- storage or distribution (Class B8)
- hotels (Class C1)
- assembly and leisure (Class D2).

Each of those may offer an opportunity in some cases. The requirement that the building be an agricultural use on 3rd July 2012 means that this change may not directly assist those with existing storage uses without permission but it may create a more positive policy climate for any applications to validate them.

6.1.3   **School/Nursery** – A new Use Class MA allows conditional rights for the change of use of a building and any land within its curtilage from use as an agricultural building (turning on its use as at 20th March 2013 – the date of the relevant announcement with that year's Budget) to use as a state-funded school or a registered nursery.

6.1.4   The full text of the legislation for these Use Classes is set out at Appendix 4 and its limitations must be noted.

6.2   Use Class MB: Conversion to Dwellings

6.2.1   Introduction – In April 2014, a new opportunity to convert existing English agricultural buildings into dwellings was created with the introduction of a new Use Class MB giving qualified permitted development rights to allow the change of use of agricultural buildings to dwellings in defined circumstances.

6.2.2   With the mix of opportunities and constraints offered by this Use Class, it may be that some will find it awkward to use this power to create the dwelling they would want. However, if only as a fallback right which may offer substantial potential in some circumstances, it may ease the process of practical discussion with the LPA over a permission for a more appropriate dwelling. The new permitted development rights appear to be a material consideration for determining a planning application.

6.2.3   The new Use Class is set out in The Town and Country Planning (General Permitted Development) (Amendment and Consequential Provisions) (England) Order 2014 (SI 2014/564). It allows the change of use of existing agricultural buildings and land within their "curtilage" to up to three dwellings, together with the building operations reasonably needed for that conversion, as permitted development. Its full text is set out at Appendix 3.

6.2.4   No conditions limiting who may occupy the resulting dwellings are imposed by the Order. Further, with no permission needed there is no opportunity for an LPA to make it conditional on a s.106 agreement.

6.2.5   These rights, subject to the qualifications reviewed below apply to buildings in or last in agricultural use on 20th March 2013. They are not limited to:
      – redundant or under-used buildings
      – traditional buildings or any particular type of construction.
They potentially allow the conversion of a Dutch barn (but see the appeal decision noted at 6.2.80 below).

6.2.6   Despite all the limitations, once the building is converted there is then no restriction, agricultural or otherwise, on who may lawfully occupy the resulting dwelling, then or in the future.

6.2.7   Where Rights are Excluded – These permitted development rights do not apply to sites (agricultural buildings and their curtilage):
      – that are listed buildings or are or contained in scheduled ancient monuments
      – on land in National Parks, AONBs, conservation areas, World Heritage Sites and the Broads (Article 1(5) areas), so excluding significant rural areas.
      – on land subject to an Article 4 direction withdrawing permitted development rights
      – in Sites of Special Scientific Interest
      – in a safety hazard area or on a military explosives storage area.
The rights do apply in Green Belt areas whose objective of resisting urban coalescence is not affected by the conversion of an existing building.

6.2.8 **Cautions** – Care should be taken in considering these permitted development rights which are much more qualified and limited than the generality of residential or agricultural permitted development rights. This text was written only months after these rights became available. Early experience (see 6.2.74-82 below) has shown widely varying reactions by local planning authorities on receiving notifications, from accepting them in the spirit that DCLG appears to have intended to requiring levels of supporting information that are almost as costly as seeking a full permission. Some still appear uncertain as to how to receive a notification.

6.2.9   On some points, the understanding of these rights has to be provisional as there has yet been no judicial interpretation of the concepts introduced by Class MB and explored in this chapter.

6.2.10   A basic point, though, is that Class MB only permits what it permits and nothing more. There is not the larger tolerance and flexibility in both drafting a planning application and on implementing it. In some cases, it may be preferable to act to secure a planning permission while aware of a potential fall back to the permitted development rights.

6.2.11   It is also important to understand that these rights are mutually exclusive with the use of rights to erect agricultural buildings without permission.

6.2.12   With all these cautions, these are, nonetheless, an important extension of development opportunities for the re-use of agricultural buildings.

6.2.13   It may equally be noted that paragraph 55, bullet 3 of the National Planning Policy Framework provides an exception to rural housing policy for the re-use of redundant or disused buildings of any sort as an isolated home where this would enhance the immediate setting.

6.2.14 **General** – The rights only apply to:
- buildings (strictly the "site" as the building with its curtilage)
- which were in agricultural use
- as part of an "established agricultural unit" on 20th March 2013 (again, the date of the relevant announcement with that year's Budget), or which were not in use on that date but had previously been in agricultural use and had not been used for any other use. Any new agricultural buildings built or changed to agricultural use after 20th March 2013 cannot take advantage of the permitted development rights until they have been in agricultural use for ten years.

Guidance – Document the use (or last previous use) of buildings as at 20th March 2013 while the necessary evidence can be assembled

6.2.15   By contrast to permitted development rights for agricultural buildings, there is no minimum size of agricultural unit for these rights.

6.2.16 **Definitions – A Building** – The 1990 Act offers a broad definition of a "building:
" "building" includes any structure or erection, and any part of a building, as so defined, but does not include plant or machinery comprised in a building;"

6.2.17   The acceptance here that a building can be part of a building appears helpful when considering using these rights to convert part of an agricultural building to a dwelling within the floor space limits allowed.

6.2.18   Where a building has fallen into decay, it will be a matter of fact as to whether it remains or has ceased to be a building.

6.2.19   **Definitions – An Agricultural Building** – This is defined to mean:
"… a building used for agriculture and which is so used for the purposes of a trade or business, and excludes any dwellinghouse, and "agricultural use" refers to such uses."
This definition was inserted into Part 3 of Schedule 2 of the original 1995 Order as part of a new Section O on interpretation of that Part by Paragraph 5 of the 2013 amending Order.

6.2.20   **Definitions – The Curtilage** – The site potentially benefiting from these rights is not just the building but also its "curtilage", so allowing a garden, parking or other area for the new dwelling. This is defined for this purpose:
" "curtilage" means, for the purposes of Class M, MA or MB only—
(i)   the piece of land, whether enclosed or unenclosed, immediately beside or around the agricultural building, closely associated with and serving the purposes of the agricultural building, or
(ii)   an area of land immediately beside or around the agricultural building no larger than the land area occupied by the agricultural building,
whichever is the lesser;".
That means that the ancillary "curtilage" to go with the new dwelling(s) cannot have a larger area than their total area and so will never be larger than 450m^2.

Guidance – Check if the layout on the ground dictates a smaller curtilage than the size of the building because of (i).

6.2.21   **Definitions – Agricultural Use** – The rights are not available where the "site" (both the building and any land within its curtilage) "was not used solely for agricultural use" on the relevant dates.

6.2.22   These rights are not available for buildings that were in other uses on 20th March 2013. They have not been introduced for previously agricultural buildings that had been put to a diversified use by that date. Thus, a building being used then for non-agricultural storage does not qualify.

6.2.23   As the building must also be an "agricultural building" (albeit not "solely") for the change from that use to be available, it seems probable that even if a building and its curtilage were then in agricultural use, as the rights are for change of use "from an agricultural building" any subsequent diversification needs to be reversed to agricultural before the rights can be exercised.

6.2.24   "Agriculture is defined by the 1990 Act:
" "agriculture" includes horticulture, fruit growing, seed growing, dairy farming, the breeding and keeping of livestock (including any creature kept for the production of food, wool, skins or fur, or for the purpose of its use in the farming of land), the use of land as grazing land, meadow land, osier land, market gardens and nursery grounds, and the use of land for woodlands where that use is ancillary to the farming of land for other agricultural purposes, and "agricultural" shall be construed accordingly;" (s.336).

6.2.25   It is not clear that "solely" is meant absolutely. Use of this word in other contexts suggests that it may allow some *de minimis* non-agricultural use in conjunction with that

47

agricultural use. In considering farm shops, there has usually been some tolerance of sales of other goods than those produced on the farm (say, to 10 per cent of goods sold) while case law on the meaning of the word "solely" in the context of relief from non-domestic rates for agricultural buildings suggests that any other use must be less than 5 per cent.

6.2.26 Either way, a farm building with any significant non-agricultural use on 20th March 2013 will not be eligible for this. Equally, where a building was vacant on that day but had previously been temporarily used for storage before falling out of use it will not qualify for Class MB rights.

6.2.27 According to the circumstances, other newly established permitted development rights may be available for diversified buildings, such as the rights to converting offices to dwellings. These are not considered here.

6.2.28 Definitions – "Established Agricultural Unit" – This is a new concept for the new Use Classes MA and MB, used for the future control and management of these new rights by reference to the business facts of March 2013.

6.2.29 It appears to have overtaken the previous innovation "original agricultural unit" used for Class M when it was first enacted in 2013. Other than the operative dates, no reason is seen for the distinction or the change in label.

6.2.30 The Town and Country Planning (General Permitted Development) Order 1995 has defined "agricultural unit" to mean:
>"agricultural land which is occupied as a unit for the purposes of agriculture, including—
>(a) any dwelling or other building on that land occupied for the purpose of farming the land by the person who occupies the unit, or
>(b) any dwelling on that land occupied by a farmworker;"

6.2.31 It also defines "agricultural land", in part by its commercial use, as:
>"land in use for agriculture and which is so used for the purposes of a trade or business, and excludes any dwellinghouse or garden".

6.2.32 The phrase "established agricultural unit" is defined in the 2014 Order:
>"established agricultural unit" means agricultural land occupied as a unit for the purposes of agriculture—
>(i)   for the purposes of Class M, on or before 3rd July 2012 or for ten years before the date the development begins; or
>(ii) for the purposes of Class MA or MB, on or before 20th March 2013 or for ten years before the date the development begins;

6.2.33 Case law has reviewed what a "planning unit" is for the application of planning policy and this has been considered in agricultural circumstances by the Court of Appeal in *Fuller* and *Wealden*. The planning unit is essentially the area occupied with the subject site.

6.2.34 Analysing the definition and that case law suggests that, for Class MB, it will for some time mean the physical area of land that was occupied as an agricultural unit on 20th March 2013. That is taken to mean land managed as a unit, not just land within one ring fence. While it is unlikely that the unit will often be larger than the farm business at that date, there will be cases where a farm business may comprise separate and distinguishable units, with different management, machinery, labour and other resources.

6.2.35   It will differ from the "planning unit" in two ways:
   – it is frozen in time
   – it will not include land that was then in non-agricultural use.

6.2.36   It would appear, therefore, that where land is subsequently acquired or otherwise brought into use by that farm business, it will not be part of the established agricultural unit for these purposes. Equally, where some of the March 2013 land is transferred it will remain part of the particular "established agricultural unit" for these rights (perhaps something to be considered in the conveyancing of any part sale).

6.2.37   It will be a question of analysis of the case in hand to identify what is regarded as the relevant "established agricultural unit" for these permitted development rights as this matters for:
   – the number of dwellings that can be developed within the rights
   – the mutual exclusion of these rights with the permitted development rights for agricultural buildings.

6.2.38   Maximum Extent of the Rights – There are two direct limits on the scale of the permitted rights within that "established agricultural unit":
   – the cumulative floor space of the existing buildings changing use under Class MB must not exceed 450m^2 (MB.1(b). The expression "floor space" suggests this may refer to the internal area within any walls rather than the building's complete footprint.
   – the cumulative number of separate dwellinghouses developed within that unit must not exceed three (MB.1(c)).

6.2.39   Both these ceilings are expressed as "cumulative" and are therefore to be assessed over time. They could though all be used at once or over several years. Once either of those ceilings is reached, these permitted development rights on that "established agricultural unit" are exhausted.

6.2.40   The limit on area is expressed in terms of floor space of the existing buildings, not of the new dwellings. The uses of "floor space" is taken mean requiring any internal floors in the agricultural building (such as for old haylofts) to be included in this assessment. However, it may also be that permitted building operations do not include providing new floor levels.

6.2.41   This is also taken as further support for the view that part only of a building can be converted – as well as several buildings – provided that overall area limit is not exceeded. Any works to the remainder of the building would not be covered by Class MB though it may be that partial demolition to enable the building operations would be allowed.

6.2.42   The limit on the number of dwellings appears to take account of all dwellings "developed" on that unit, whether under these permitted development rights or otherwise. Thus, if a separate permission is gained for a new build worker's cottage or a farmhouse that will use up one of the three dwellings permitted, even though there has been no conversion of an agricultural building. That would suggest that, where part of the "established agricultural unit" is sold and developed for housing, that could of itself exhaust these rights.

6.2.43   It seems probable from the context that this means three dwellings developed since 20th March 2013, rather than looking back further.

6.2.44 Specific Restrictions on the Conversion – There are a number of significant restrictions on the implementation of any conversion under these rights that may mean that this option will not suit every farm building.

6.2.45   No changes can be made which would result in the external dimensions of the converted building being larger than the external dimensions of the original building at any point (MB.1(g)). This means that no part of the new dwelling can extend beyond the previous building. New chimneys, flues or porches cannot go outside that envelope. That may impose a significant practical constraint.

6.2.46   Overall, the cumulative development under these rights is not to result in more than 450m² of floor space of buildings changing use within an established agricultural unit (MB.1(h)). It is not clear how this differs in meaning from the limit under MB.1(b)) reviewed above. The words here do not seem to limit the floor space of the new dwellings.

6.2.47   The building operations permitted by these rights are limited to:
  – the installation or replacement of doors, windows, roofs or external walls. The acceptance that external walls can be installed means that open sided buildings can benefit from Class MB – provided that the new development does not extend outside the external dimensions of the agricultural building.
  – the installation or replacement of water, gas, electricity, drainage or other services
  – such partial demolition as necessary to carry out those building operations (MB.1(i)).

6.2.48   Bats – While planning permission is not needed for this conversion, that does not lift the regime protecting bats and their roosts.

6.2.49   Mutual Exclusion with Permitted Development Rights for Agricultural Buildings – There are longstanding permitted development rights to:
  – erect, extend or alter an agricultural building on an agricultural unit of 5 ha or more
  – extend or alter an agricultural building on an agricultural unit of not less 0.4 ha.
where reasonably necessary for the purposes of agriculture within that unit but subject to conditions, including a maximum area of 465m² in a two year period.

6.2.50   However, permitted development rights under Class MB are mutually exclusive with these building rights. Exercising either of these two classes of rights since 20th March 2013 within the "established agricultural unit" excludes use of the other on that unit for the following ten years (MB.1(f)).

6.2.51   One point that remains to be checked is whether work within permitted development rights for an agricultural building which commenced before 20th March 2013 but was not completed until after that date excludes use of Class MB. It is suggested that provided the exercise of permitted development rights began before that date Class MB may not be excluded but this cannot be a definitive view. It may equally be a matter of interpretation as to when such a building was completed. However, if the new building was erected under a planning permission then it will not affect access to Class MB rights. Either way, if it was in agricultural use before 20th March 2013 then it could itself benefit from Class MB but not if it was not brought into agricultural use until later.

6.2.52   It should be noted that *altering* an agricultural building is an action within permitted development rights and so if done after 20th March 2013 would serve to exclude all Class MB rights for dwellings on the agricultural unit as it was on at that date until ten years after that alteration. Where there is an intention to use MB rights, it would be prudent to review whether there have been any such alterations or, if they are in mind, to consider seeking planning permission to do them.

6.2.53   It seems unlikely that securing retrospective planning permission for a building that that had been erected under permitted development would remove the exclusion of Class MB rights.

6.2.54   While many new agricultural buildings may be larger than the historic limit (set in 1960) of 465m² and so need permission as will many buildings for intensive livestock, this is nonetheless an issue to consider when making decisions about either farm buildings or the use of Class MB rights. It might be that an active and expanding agricultural business would prefer to keep the operational benefit of permitted development rights for further buildings than to take advantage of the opportunity to convert a building into a dwelling.

6.2.55   This could become more of an issue as parts of the "established agricultural unit" change hands, whether by sale, inheritance or the termination or grant of tenancies, not only taking any restriction with them but also apparently continuing to interact for this exclusion. Thus, if a new owner of some old buildings sold away after 20th March 2013 used Class MB rights to convert them into dwellings that appears to exclude the owner of the remaining land from having permitted development rights to erect or extend an agricultural building.

6.2.56   However, if more land is added to the business that new land would not be bound.

6.2.57   No Further Permitted Development Rights for the Dwellings – None of usual permitted development rights for dwellings, including minor extensions such as porches, are to be available to a dwelling created under Class MB.

6.2.58   Interaction with Existing Planning Permissions – What might be the position where there is an unimplemented planning permission for conversion to holiday lets? That might need to be tested as at 20th March 2013 or a later date. Where steps have been taken to commence implementation – to keep the permission alive for the longer term – that may pose a hurdle in showing that the building was still in agricultural use. Consideration may be given to applying for a variation to the permission to allow residential use.

Guidance – Before undertaking any development within the permitted development regime for agricultural buildings consider the implications here.

6.2.59   Where the Buildings are or were within an Agricultural Tenancy – Where the buildings and its curtilage (the site) are within a current tenancy under either the Agricultural Holdings Act 1986 or the Agricultural Tenancies Act 1995 (an agricultural tenancy), both landlord and tenant must have consented in writing to the proposed change of use (MB.1(d)).

6.2.60   It is possible that there may be circumstances where it will suit both parties for such a development to take place within a tenancy – perhaps to provide necessary accommodation for farm staff, the tenant's family or to enable a succession. The question of which party does this, how it is funded between them, subsequent rental, repairing, insuring and compensation terms should be considered and agreed as should any basis for the occupation of the new dwelling.

6.2.61 Where such an agricultural tenancy of the site was terminated less than 12 months before the development begins and the termination was for the purpose of carrying out the development, then the development is not permitted unless both landlord and tenant have agreed in writing that the site is no longer required for agricultural use (MB.1(e)). In a conventional 1986 Act tenancy or an FBT that, in practice, is likely to impose a delay of over two years before Class MB rights are available without the tenant's written agreement.

6.2.62 Case B? – While the exercise of any break clause for development (or other purposes) in an FBT will be regulated by the tenancy agreement, the wording of Case B is taken to exclude the possibility of using permitted development rights (rather than a planning permission) for a landlord to serve an "incontestable" notice to quit under the 1986 Act. The circumstances in which an enforceable Case B notice to quit does not turn on planning permission were redefined in 1990 to be:

- land required for non-agricultural use for which planning permission is granted by a general development order by reason only of the fact that the use being permitted is authorised by a private or local Act of Parliament, an order of both Houses or an order made under ss.14 or 16 of the Harbours Act 1964. In practice and at present, this only applies to Part 11 of Schedule 2 to the General Permitted Development Order 1995 and so does not cover the Class MB development considered here.
- where land required for a non-agricultural use that is deemed to have planning permission by any Parliamentary provision that does not form part of the enactments for town and country planning.
- where land is required for a non-agricultural purpose which an Act, other than one that is part of town and country planning legislation, deems not be "development" and so does not need planning permission.
- where permission is not required by town and country planning legislation because of Crown immunity, now probably of very limited consequence with the extension of planning control to the Crown by the Planning and Compulsory Purchase Act 2004.

6.2.63 Otherwise – Where repossession for the purposes of carrying out the development is gained by agreement or under other grounds (including s.27(3)(f) of the 1986 Act), development under Class MB could still not be undertaken within 12 months unless both landlord and former tenant agree that the site is no longer required for agricultural use.

6.2.64 However, where possession is obtained without that motive, as after the expiry of an FBT or a notice after the tenant's death, then that condition does not apply. Ultimately, that distinction will be a matter for proof.

6.2.65 None of these restrictions apply where the site is or was in a tenancy under any other code, business, residential or common law, even though it would have to have been an agricultural building for Class MB rights to be available.

6.2.66 If In Doubt – This review has noted a number of areas where it may not be clear in a particular case whether Class MB is available or applies. It may then be appropriate to consider applying for a Certificate of Lawfulness of Proposed Use or Development under s.192 of the 1990 Act. That application will need to include sufficient information for the Local Planning Authority to reach a view.

6.2.67 Procedure – Before starting work, the local planning authority must be asked for a determination as to whether its prior approval is needed for
- transport and highways impacts
- noise impacts
- contamination risks on the site
- flooding risks on the site
- whether the location or siting of the building makes it otherwise impractical or undesirable for the building to change from an agricultural use to that of a dwellinghouse within Class C3 (up to six residents living as a single household).

6.2.68   Conditions can only be imposed if they are relevant to these issues ("reasonably related to the subject matter of the prior approval"). That makes it unlikely that they can be used to impose conditions as to occupancy or barring sale of the dwelling away from the holding.

6.2.69   A similar application must be made for a determination as to whether prior approval is required for the building's design and external appearance.

6.2.70   These applications are to follow the general procedures for prior notification.

6.2.71   The change of use can then be carried out within three years of the earlier of either:
- prior approval being granted for it or
- the notification period expiring without the planning authority giving or refusing approval.

6.2.72 Subsequent Sale – Once the development is complete, there is no bar on subsequent letting or disposal. It will be for the farmer to judge if a third party neighbour in that situation is desirable or not.

6.2.73   It would also appear that the site could be sold as a development plot provided that it was in or last in agricultural use on 20th March 2013 and is an agricultural building before the change of use. That would have the usual consequences for Class MB rights on the remainder of the March 2013 agricultural unit.

6.2.74 Early Experience of Class MB – At the time of writing Class MB has been in place for barely seven months with only that limited opportunity for applicants, advisers and LPAs to understand it and accustom themselves to its definition and processes. However, there is some limited initial experience of notifications and the first appeals over LPA reactions to those notifications. Given the inevitable issues that arise with the introduction of such a new but qualified opportunity, care should be taken in interpreting the small numbers of cases while waiting for experience on all sides to grow and consolidate. We are grateful to David Collier for his assistance in this early review.

6.2.75   In the first quarter (April to June 2014) in which Class MB was available, 52 per cent of notifications were dismissed by LPAs. Anecdote suggests different experiences with different LPAs but some of this may be subjective. Some LPAs that were rumoured to have refused all notifications are shown to have had none made to them in that quarter

– although there were early reports of some LPAs finding it difficult to register them. The statistics do show some to have refused all put to them; others have accepted all or the great majority put to them. In each case, this only concerns relatively small numbers and it is too early, at the time of writing, for these first figures to have much meaning. It may be as significant that half of notifications are not dismissed.

6.2.76   Details have been seen of four of the first appeals over notifications under Class MB.

6.2.77   The first appeal concerned one of the earliest notifications made to Harrogate Borough Council in early April 2014. It was refused in late May, and the appeal was decided on 30 September. Mr Dale wanted to convert a two-storey agricultural building into a dwelling with integral double garage some 600m outside a village. The inspector found that the site was isolated in open countryside and the building "in a dilapidated condition with a number of walls and the majority of its roof missing", "deteriorating and in an unattractive condition". He did *not* conclude that the works needed would go beyond those permitted by the Order but that, while the alterations would result in an improvement in the appearance of the building itself, there would be a greater impact on the surrounding countryside as a consequence of the proposed curtilage – with enclosing fences or hedges, patio areas and other hard surfacing and domestic paraphernalia – and the required improvements to the access track. The development would be "incongruous and not in keeping with the strong, rugged rural, unspoiled and undeveloped landscape that can be seen from long-distance views." With no special circumstances to justify the isolated countryside location of the building, the appeal was dismissed.

6.2.78   In the second appeal, Mrs Wilkin wanted to convert a building used to stable her horses, within a village, into a dwelling. She applied in late April to Mid-Suffolk District Council which decided in late June that the building was ineligible. The Inspector agreed, pointing out in his decision letter of 7th October that development is not permitted by Class MB where the site was not used solely for agricultural use, as part of an agricultural unit, on 20 March 2013. Mrs Wilkin had been candid in admitting that the building was not used for a trade or business. The horses grazed there from time to time were her own horses that were kept elsewhere and only occasionally brought to the appeal site. The Inspector therefore had no difficulty in finding that the subject building did not fall within the definition of "agricultural building" set out in the Order, so it could not benefit from the permission granted by Class MB. It was not necessary to consider whether the *land* was used solely for an agricultural use as part of an established agricultural unit on the operative date. The appeal was dismissed.

6.2.79   The third appeal relates to a notification for the conversion of a stone barn 1.8km outside Kirby Lonsdale. South Lakeland District Council, concerned at its isolated location, had rejected it on the grounds that the building works needed went beyond those permitted by the Order and the visual impact of the improvements needed to the access track. The notification was submitted in mid-April and refused in mid-June; the Inspector's decision is dated 15 October. The Inspector described the barn as "vacant and generally dilapidated", "in a state of disrepair and significant parts of its walls and roof have collapsed". That was not found to be an obstacle as paragraph MB1(i) allows building operations including the installation or replacement of windows, doors, roofs or exterior walls to the extent reasonably necessary for the building to function as a dwelling house. However, the Inspector then had regard to paragraph 17 of the NPPF, which sets out the core planning principle of recognising the intrinsic character and beauty of the countryside and supporting thriving rural communities within it; and to paragraph 55, which advised LPAs to avoid new isolated homes in the countryside unless there are special circumstances. The building "sits in a field remote from the main road, the nearest settlement is 1.8km away and reached across fields and the A65", the site was a "considerable distance" from important local services and the surroundings had an open character. While the converted barn might be more attractive than it was in its present run-down condition, there would be a greater impact on the surrounding countryside. A residential curtilage with parking, hard surfacing, enclosures and domestic paraphernalia would all be "visually intrusive in the landscape and appear at odds with the surrounding rural character of the open fields". The track needed to give access to A65 was not evident where it crossed the open fields. The improved track would be visible in the surrounding countryside, adding to the proposal's urbanising effect on the rural character of the area. The visual impact would not be significantly reduced by conditions. The development would not enhance the immediate setting of the barn – the key element of paragraph 55 emphasised by the appellant – but would harm the surrounding countryside. With no special circumstances to justify the isolated countryside location of the building, it would be *undesirable* for the appeal building to become a dwelling house, and it accordingly failed to comply with the MB requirements. The Inspector also rejected an argument that the scheme would increase rural housing as its contribution to the housing stock would be too small to outweigh the harm caused.

6.2.80 The fourth of these early appeal decisions concerns the proposed conversion of a metal-clad Dutch barn with associated lean-to buildings in Devon into a dwelling house. Mr and Mrs Stone were living in temporary accommodation and wanted to live on their land in a permanent dwelling; they were willing to accept an agricultural occupancy condition. They applied in early April and Teignbridge District Council turned them down in early July. The Inspector found that the buildings generally were dilapidated and the barn itself was in "poor condition". The site was "in an isolated location in the countryside with access to the nearest village along narrow, mainly single-track lanes which lack public transport and are unlit". Facilities such as shops and schools and a bus service in local villages were "some distance away" in villages that were "themselves remote from the larger centres of population where a larger range of services is found and that the site is in an unsustainable location for a dwelling where the occupants would be reliant on private motor vehicles for transport." The appellants had failed to detail the building operations required to effect the conversion. The Inspector felt that "some consideration of the amount of such operations likely to be required is relevant in determining the practicality of the proposal". She was not convinced that the existing structural framework was substantial enough to be capable of conversion to a dwelling which would meet modern standards, without needing a degree of demolition and construction which would amount to a new building with very little of the original left. The proposal was unacceptable because it would be "impractical and undesirable because of its location … I consider that the appellants have not demonstrated an essential need for the dwelling in terms of the nature or viability of their business sufficient to overcome the objection arising from the isolated location." Being impractical and undesirable, it would not meet condition MB.2(e) of the Order.

6.2.81 Reviewing these four lost appeals:
- the Suffolk building was simply ineligible
- the Teignbridge case failed on its location being found unsustainable and an inadequate justification as to the works and need.
- the Kirby Lonsdale and Harrogate cases failed on a combination of domestic paraphernalia and a longer access track

6.2.82   This handful of early appeals suggests some potential lessons:
   (i)   If the location can be described as isolated countryside
      – good reason may be needed to overcome objections based on the NPPF's paragraph 55
      – concerns about the visual impact of the change of use along with associated 'domestic paraphernalia' may mark it out as unsustainable development.
   (ii) In some cases the LPA and the Inspector on appeal may conclude that the location is unsustainable primarily because there would be reliance on private transport; this alone would rule out a lot of farmsteads.
   (iii) Noting the two appeals above that failed in part on their access tracks, if the appearance of an improved access track is likely to be controversial, an applicant might be prudent to consider putting the access track for the site into an acceptable condition before submitting the notification so minimising the proposed conversion's impact on the landscape.
   (iv) The building must be an agricultural building on the relevant date. This is unlikely in practice to be shown for stables in equestrian use.
   (v)   An argument that the conversion will add to the housing stock will carry little weight, and on its own will be insufficient to overcome objections to an isolated location.
   (vi) While the Order does permit quite extensive building works, these should be properly described to avoid a conclusion that the works amount to demolition and complete rebuilding.

7. RURAL WORKERS' DWELLINGS IN WALES

7.1   Devolution and Planning

7.1.1   The primary legislation governing development control in Wales has been the same as that in England and so for this paper the Town and Country Planning Act 1990, the Planning and Compulsory Purchase Act 2004 and much of the Localism Act 2011 apply. However, the Planning (Wales) Bill was published in October 2014 but awaited all its legislative stages and a further more comprehensive statute was foreshadowed.

7.1.2   Since its creation the Assembly has had the power to make statutory instruments for development control in Wales and so has made its own changes to the General Permitted Development Orders, for example, since 2002. These do not necessarily follow changes in England and, in particular, there is no equivalent to the new English Use Class MB for the conversion of agricultural buildings to dwellings.

7.1.3   Schedule 7 to the Government of Wales Act 2006 at paragraph 18 gives the Welsh Assembly the power to make statutes governing:
> *"Town and country planning*
> "Town and country planning, including listed buildings and conservation areas. Caravan sites. Spatial planning. Mineral workings. Urban development. New towns. Protection of visual amenity.
> *"Exception* — Functions of the Infrastructure Planning Commission or any of its members under the Planning Act 2008."

This power has been available since 2011 and may perhaps be construed broadly in the light of the Supreme Court's decision in *Agriculture Sector (Wales) Bill Reference by the Attorney General for England and Wales*. It is now being used to bring the Planning (Wales) Bill forward.

7.1.4   Policy – The Welsh Government is responsible for ordinary development control policy in Wales, issuing its own guidance notes and other advice for Local Planning Authorities (LPAs) in Wales to take into account.

7.1.5   The general framework for planning policy in Wales is set out in Planning Policy Wales (PPW) which, with circulars and Technical Advice Notes (TANs):
– is to be taken into account as LPAs prepare development plans
– may be material to decisions on individual planning applications
– will be taken into account by Welsh Ministers and planning inspectors when determining applications that have been called in and appeals.

The English National Planning Policy Framework does not apply in Wales. The new Planning (Wales) Bill is to provide for a National Development Framework.

7.1.6   The Welsh Government's planning guidance is largely issued in Technical Advice Notes (TANs). For the purposes of this paper TAN 6, Planning for Sustainable Rural Communities, is the basic document outlining exceptions to a bar on residential development in open countryside, issued in July 2010. That TAN replaced its previous version, Agriculture and Rural Development issued in June 2000.

7.1.7   TAN 6 has since been supplemented by Practice Guidance – Rural Enterprise Dwellings, issued in December 2011.

7.2 Planning Policy Wales

7.2.1 Edition 6 of this policy guidance was issued in February 2014 as a 211 page electronic document:
- providing an overview of the planning system in Wales and its principal procedures.
- setting out the main policy objectives and principles which underpin the application to particular subjects.
- stating the Welsh Government's objectives and how the subjects should be treated in development plans and for development management purposes.
- Giving a guide to the application of national planning policy statements in Local Development Plans.

7.2.2 Its para 4.6.3 sets priorities for rural areas as to secure:
"• sustainable rural communities with access to affordable housing and high quality public services;
• a thriving and diverse local economy where agriculture-related activities are complemented by sustainable tourism and other forms of employment in a working countryside; and
• an attractive, ecologically rich and accessible countryside in which the environment and biodiversity are conserved and enhanced."

7.2.3 Its general policy on development in open countryside is at para 4.7.8
"**Development in the countryside** should be located within and adjoining those settlements where it can be best be accommodated in terms of infrastructure, access and habitat and landscape conservation. Infilling or minor extensions to existing settlements may be acceptable, in particular where it meets a local need for affordable housing, but new building in the open countryside away from existing settlements or areas allocated for development in development plans must continue to be strictly controlled. All new development should respect the character of the surrounding area and should be of appropriate scale and design."

7.2.4 The framework for rural housing policy is set out at 9.2.22:
"In planning for **housing in rural areas** it is important to recognise that development in the countryside should embody sustainability principles, benefiting the rural economy and local communities while maintaining and enhancing the environment. There should be a choice of housing, recognising the housing needs of all, including those in need of affordable or special needs provision. In order to safeguard the character and appearance of the countryside, to reduce the need to travel by car and to economise on the provision of services, new houses in the countryside, away from existing settlements recognised in development plans or from other areas allocated for development, must be strictly controlled. Many parts of the countryside have isolated groups of dwellings. Sensitive filling in of small gaps, or minor extensions to such groups, in particular for affordable housing to meet local need, may be acceptable, but much depends upon the character of the surroundings, the pattern of development in the area and the accessibility to main towns and villages."

7.2.5 Policies for housing in the open countryside, whether for rural enterprise dwellings or as One Planet Development are covered in the paragraphs from 9.3.6:
"9.3.6 New house building and other new development in the open countryside, away from established settlements, should be strictly controlled. The fact that a single house on a particular site would be unobtrusive is not, by itself, a good argument in favour of permission; such permissions could be granted too often, to

the overall detriment of the character of an area. Isolated new houses in the open countryside require special justification, for example where they are essential to enable rural enterprise workers to live at or close to their place of work in the absence of nearby accommodation. All applications for new rural enterprise dwellings should be carefully examined to ensure that there is a genuine need. It will be important to establish whether the rural enterprise is operating as a business and will continue to operate for a reasonable length of time. New rural enterprise dwellings should be located within or adjoining the existing farm/business complex or access. Local planning authorities should follow the guidance in TAN 6 with regard to the requirements for rural enterprise dwelling appraisals.

"9.3.7 The Welsh Government wishes to encourage younger people to manage farm businesses and promote the diversification of established farms. To support this policy objective it may be appropriate to allow a second dwelling on established farms that are financially sustainable in the following situations:

- Where there are secure and legally binding arrangements in place to demonstrate that management of the farm business has been transferred to a person younger than the person currently responsible for management, or, that transfer of management is only conditional upon grant of planning permission for the dwelling. The younger person should demonstrate majority control over the farm business and be the decision maker for the farm business partnership; or
- Where there is an existing functional need for an additional 0.5 or more of a full-time worker and that person obtains at least 50% of a Grade 2 Standard Worker salary (as defined by the latest version of the Agricultural Wages Order), from the farm business.

In these circumstances a rural enterprise dwelling may be considered favourably provided the criteria set out above and in TAN 6 paragraph 4.4.1 (c) – (e) are met. These special policy exceptions will only apply to the first additional dwelling to be attached to an established farm after TAN 6 comes into force and **not to subsequent dwellings**.

"9.3.8 It is important to establish that stated intentions to engage in the rural enterprise are genuine, are reasonably likely to materialise and are capable of being sustained for a reasonable period. If it is considered that a new dwelling will be essential to support a new rural enterprise, but the case is not completely proven, the dwelling should normally for the first three years be a caravan, or a wooden structure which can be easily dismantled, or other temporary accommodation. Temporary rural enterprise dwellings should satisfy normal planning requirements, for example on siting and access, and will have to be removed at the end of the period for which the permission was granted. Local planning authorities should not grant temporary planning permissions in locations where they would not permit a permanent dwelling.

"9.3.9 Where the need to provide accommodation to enable a rural enterprise worker to live at or near their place of work has been accepted as justifying isolated residential development in the open countryside, it will be necessary to ensure that the dwellings are kept available for this need. For this reason planning permission should be granted subject to an occupancy condition. Rural enterprise dwellings should also be classified as affordable housing as defined in TAN 2, *Planning and Affordable Housing*. This will ensure that the dwelling remains available to meet local affordable housing need should the original justification have ceased to exist.

"9.3.10 Applications for rural enterprise dwellings must only be permitted where the rural enterprise dwelling appraisal provides conclusive evidence of the need for the dwelling and an occupancy condition is applied.

"9.3.11 **One Planet Development** is development that through its low impact either enhances or does not significantly diminish environmental quality. One Planet Developments should initially achieve an ecological footprint of 2.4 global hectares per person or less in terms of consumption and demonstrate clear potential to move towards 1.88 global hectares over time (the global average availability of resources in 2003). They should also be zero carbon in both construction and use.

"9.3.12 One Planet Developments may take a number of forms. They can either be single homes, co-operative communities or larger settlements. They may be located within or adjacent to existing settlements or be situated in the open countryside. **Land based One Planet Developments located in the open countryside** should provide for the minimum needs of the inhabitants in terms of income, food, energy and waste assimilation over a period of no more than 5 years from the commencement of work on the site. This should be evidenced by a management plan produced by a competent person(s). The management plan should set out the objectives of the proposal, the timetable for development of the site and the timescale for review. It should be used as the basis of a legal agreement relating to the occupation of the site, should planning consent be granted."

7.3   TAN 6
7.3.1   General – This guidance outlines in more detail Welsh Government policy on:
    – rural communities
    – the rural economy
    – rural housing, including "rural enterprise dwellings"
    – rural services
    – agriculture
placing its focus on achieving "sustainable rural communities", judged in economic, social and environmental terms. For housing, it is to be read in conjunction with TAN 2, Planning and Affordable Housing.

7.3.2   There is a stated theme that:
    "Planning authorities should seek to strengthen rural communities by helping to ensure that existing residents can work and access services locally using low carbon travel and obtain a higher proportion of their energy needs from local renewable sources." (Para 2.1.1)

7.3.3   A distinction is suggested between development in general and development to meet local needs. TAN 6 advises:
    "Where possible existing definitions of local need, for example affordable housing to meet local need, should be adopted, or if necessary modified to include other land uses.

    "Where development proposals are intended to meet local needs, planning authorities should recognise that a site may be acceptable even though it may not be accessible other than by the private car." (Paras 2.2.2 and 2.2.3)

7.3.4   Otherwise, development is to be in market towns and their settlements where "a sustainable functional linkage can be demonstrated and which are accessible by public transport". Thus, development justified by local needs is not so constrained.

7.3.5 **The Welsh Rural Economy** – TAN 6 recognises that:

"Many businesses in rural areas are small, with self employment being common place. The business is often operated from home, providing a sustainable business model. Planning authorities should encourage the growth of self employment and micro businesses by adopting a supportive approach to home based work. Planning applications for employment premises at home should be supported provided local amenity is not compromised to an unacceptable degree. Development plans should identify new opportunities for home/ work developments." (para 3.1.4)

Further:

"Many economic activities can be sustainably located on farms. Small on-farm operations such as food and timber processing and food packing, together with services (e.g. offices, workshop facilities, equipment hire and maintenance), sports and recreation services, and the production of non-food crops and renewable energy, are likely to be appropriate uses."

7.4 Rural Enterprise Dwellings

7.4.1 TAN 6 has perhaps been most noted for expressly developing a policy for "rural enterprise dwellings" as an exception to general policy against "new isolated development in the open countryside" at para 4.3.1:

"One of the few circumstances in which new isolated residential development in the open countryside may be justified is when accommodation is required to enable rural enterprise workers to live at, or close to, their place of work. Whether this is essential in any particular case will depend on the needs of the rural enterprise concerned and not on the personal preference or circumstances of any of the individuals involved. Applications for planning permission for new rural enterprise dwellings should be carefully assessed by the planning authority to ensure that a departure from the usual policy of restricting development in the open countryside can be fully justified by reference to robust supporting evidence.

"Rural enterprise dwellings include:
- A new dwelling on an established rural enterprise (including farms) where there is a functional need for a full time worker and the business case demonstrates that the employment is likely to remain financially sustainable. (See paragraph 4.4.1).
- A second dwelling on an established farm which is financially sustainable, to facilitate the handover of the management of the farm business to a younger farmer. (See paragraphs 4.5.1 – 4.5.3).
- A second dwelling on an established farm which is financially sustainable, where there is a functional need for a further 0.5 or more of a full time worker and at least 50% of a Grade 2 Standard Worker salary, as defined by the latest version of the Agricultural Wages Order, is obtained from the farm business. (See paragraphs 4.5.1 – 4.5.3).
- A new dwelling on a new rural enterprise where there is a functional need for a full time worker and the criteria in paragraphs 4.5.3 a-e are fully evidenced. (See paragraphs 4.6.1 – 4.6.2)."

7.4.2 Further detail is given on:
- what qualifies as a "rural enterprise"
- new dwellings for established rural enterprises
- second dwellings on established farms
- new dwellings on new enterprises

and the appraisals and tests that are required.

61

7.4.3 Permission for such a dwelling should be made subject to a new occupancy condition (Para 4.13.1) which might also be applied to other dwellings in the business.

7.4.4 Permissions under this policy require there to be a "**rural enterprise**". This is defined in terms of land-based businesses such as agriculture and forestry, land management work and tourism and leisure with the freedom for local development plans to broaden this. Para 4.3.2 states:

"For the purpose of this technical advice note qualifying rural enterprises comprise land related businesses including agriculture, forestry and other activities that obtain their primary inputs from the site, such as the processing of agricultural, forestry and mineral products together with land management activities and support services (including agricultural contracting), tourism and leisure enterprises. Development plans may include a broader definition of qualifying rural enterprises where this can be justified by specific local evidence."

7.4.5 The Practice Guidance Paper of December 2011 puts it simply:
"This extension applies primarily to land-related businesses which, directly or indirectly, need to be located in the countryside rather than in existing settlements." (Para 1.7)

7.4.6 This is thus a much broader policy than the traditional one that made exceptions for just agriculture and forestry. The Practice Guidance allows that this includes "the exploitation of mineral and water resources and other forms of land management" (Para 2.4) and could include "substantive equine and fishery enterprises, kennels, catteries and veterinary facilities" (Para 2.5). Para 2.6 continues to advise that where there is a strong degree of interaction of on-site processing of primary production with the land management (as with making cheese on dairy farm) that could also potentially qualify. Para 2.7 expresses caution about general services to land management (such as building maintenance or professional services) compared to practical services such as relief labour, land management contracting (silaging, fencing, walling), veterinary or farriery services. More definitively, Para 2.8 accepts that circumstances may arise where key elements of the workforce for tourism, leisure and conservation need to be appropriately housed close to their work in the countryside.

7.4.7 The Practice Guidance offers a summary of key points:
   – "The scope of the rural enterprise dwelling policy relates to enterprises which, by their inherent nature or the services they provide, can only be located in the countryside or can provide special justification for such a location.
   – "Only where the enterprise has an essential functional need for the close supervision by a worker and is appropriately located in the countryside will a housing proposal fall within the scope of the policy.
   – "Qualifying proposals must fall within one of four specific circumstances identified in the policy.
   – "Proposals arising from personal preferences or circumstances, or for conditions of convenience rather than essential need, will not qualify within the policy."

7.4.8 Five tests are set for **new buildings on established new enterprises** by para 4.4:
"New permanent dwellings should only be allowed to support established rural enterprises providing:
a. there is a clearly established *existing* functional need; (See paragraph 4.8.1).

b. the need relates to a *full-time* worker, and does not relate to a part-time requirement; (See paragraph 4.7.1) (See paragraphs 4.5.1 – 4.5.3 for policy exemptions).

c. the enterprise concerned has been established for at least three years, profitable for at least one of them and both the enterprise and the business need for the job, is currently financially sound, and has a clear prospect of remaining so; (See paragraphs 4.10.1 – 4.10.3).

d. the functional need could not be fulfilled by another dwelling or by converting an existing suitable building already on the land holding comprising the enterprise, or any other existing accommodation in the locality which is suitable and available for occupation by the worker concerned; (See paragraphs 4.11.1 – 4.11.2),and

e. other normal planning requirements, for example siting and access, are satisfied. (See paragraphs 4.12.1 – 4.12.2)."

7.4.9   There is a particular recognition of the case for a **first additional dwelling on an established farm** to aid the handover of such businesses to younger farmers. There is no requirement that this be within the family and so could support a variety of situations including perhaps the letting of the farm.

7.4.10   This is effectively a broadening of the general policy for new dwellings on established enterprises. The five tests set out for that still apply subject either of two alternative points:

– majority control of the business has been transferred to the younger person

– while the full time worker requirement is relaxed there must be a functional need for at least half a worker.

7.4.11   Para 4.5.1 says:

"The Assembly Government wishes to encourage younger people to manage farm businesses and promote the diversification of established farms. To support this policy objective it may be appropriate to allow a second dwelling on established farms that are financially sustainable where the criteria set out in paragraph 4.4.1 cannot be fully satisfied. The two exceptions to the policy are:

• Where there are secure and legally binding arrangements in place to demonstrate that management of the farm business has been transferred to a person younger than the person currently responsible for management, or, that transfer of management is only conditional upon grant of planning permission for the dwelling. The younger person should demonstrate majority control over the farm business and be the decision maker for the farm business; or,

• There is an existing functional need for an additional 0.5 or more of a full time worker and that person obtains at least 50% of a Grade 2 Standard Worker salary, (as defined by the latest version of the Agricultural Wages Order), from the farm business."

7.4.12   Para 4.5.3 requires that:

"It must also be demonstrated that the management successor or part time worker is critical to the continued success of the farm business, and that the need cannot be met in any other reasonable way, e.g. through the re-organisation of labour responsibilities. In addition, where all the criteria specified above are met the planning authority should ensure that the new dwelling is tied to the holding by way of a legal agreement."

7.4.13 This broadening of the general policy for new dwellings on established businesses is only available for the first additional dwelling created after the new TAN 6 came into force in July 2010. (Para 4.5.2)

7.4.14 The Practice Guidance confirms that there will need to be legally binding documentary evidence to demonstrate that the majority control of the business has indeed been transferred to the younger person concerned (Para 8.2) to prevent abuse of this relaxation of planning policy. It recognises that there is no simple universal means for doing this and that it will require professional support and consideration of the long term trading and taxation implications but suggests that means to achieve the end include:
- re-apportioning administrative and operational responsibilities and final rewards and liabilities in a partnership or limited company
- granting control of the productive assets of a farm by a gift, tenancy or contract agreement with younger person (Para 8.8).

Such evidence could also, as appropriate, be relevant to a claim for the Young Farmer top up payment under the CAP direct payments regime from 2015.

7.4.15 Specific guidance is then given on the difficult subject of **new dwellings on new enterprises** for which much evidence is required to show that the enterprise and dwelling are warranted functionally and financially.

7.4.16 Para 4.6.1 outlines the approach to this with six criteria:
"If it is considered that a new dwelling will be essential to support a new rural enterprise, it should satisfy the following criteria:
a. clear evidence of a firm intention and ability to develop the rural enterprise concerned (significant investment in new buildings and equipment is often a good indication of intentions);
b. clear evidence that the new enterprise needs to be established at the proposed location and that it cannot be accommodated at another suitable site where a dwelling is likely to be available;
c. clear evidence that the proposed enterprise has been planned on a sound financial basis;
d. there is a clearly established functional need and that need relates to a *full-time* worker, and does not relate to a part-time requirement;
e. the functional need could not be fulfilled by another dwelling or by converting an existing suitable building on the enterprise, or any other existing accommodation in the locality which is suitable and available for occupation by the workers concerned; and
f. other normal planning requirements, for example siting and access, are satisfied.

7.4.17 Para 4.6.2 accepts that where the case for a permanent dwelling cannot be fully made, the position can be handled by a temporary permission, commonly for three years, after which the dwelling should be removed. It sets a bias against renewing temporary permissions but asks the LPA to state the requirements to be met for a permanent permission to be given later.

7.5   Rural Enterprise Dwelling Appraisals
Note – An illustrative framework for such appraisals is offered at Appendix 6.
7.5.1   Robust evidence is expected to support any application for such a dwelling. An appraisal is to accompany each application with:
"information sufficient to enable the planning authority to make a full and effective assessment."

A framework for such an appraisal is offered at Appendix 6 as a prompt to thought, not as an exhaustive model.

7.5.2   After a full description of the operation and management of the rural enterprise (Practice Guidance 3.9.2) the Rural Enterprise Dwelling Appraisal is to address five points outlined at para 4.7.1:

> "• The *functional test* to provide evidence of whether there is a need for a resident worker for the proper functioning of the enterprise. (See paragraph 4.8.1).
>
> • The *time test* to provide evidence of the labour requirement for the worker who is working on the justifying enterprise. (See paragraphs 4.9.1).
>
> • The *financial test* to provide evidence of the economic sustainability of the justifying enterprise and identify the size of dwelling that the enterprise can sustain, ensuring that the size of the dwelling is commensurate with its functional need and financial justification. (See paragraphs 4.10.1 – 4.10.3).
>
> • The *other dwellings test* to identify whether there is an existing dwelling or building suitable for conversion on the enterprise or dwelling in the locality that could meet the identified functional need. (See paragraphs 4.11.1 – 4.11.2).
>
> • *Other normal planning requirements test* to demonstrate that the dwelling is suitably located to fulfil its identified need and to minimise impact on the wider environment. (See paragraphs 4.12.1 – 4.12.2)."

Where an application is for an additional dwelling to facilitate succession in the management of a farm the necessary information regarding the relevant tests should also be covered.

7.5.3   TAN 6 then gives further guidance on each of these main five tests. Each of these is then further developed in the Practice Guidance issued in December 2011.

7.5.4   Where available, it has been found useful to stay in touch with the person used by the LPA to advise on such applications.

7.5.5   The Functional Test – The first test for TAN 6 is to establish whether it is essential for workers to be readily available with particular scrutiny where there are already dwellings on site:

> "4.8.1 A *functional test* is necessary to establish whether it is essential, for the proper functioning of the enterprise, for one or more workers to be readily available at most times. It should relate to unexpected situations that might arise, for which workers are needed to be on hand outside of normal working hours for the particular enterprise. Such requirements might arise, for example, if workers are needed to be on hand night and day to deal with an emergency that would threaten the continued viability and existence of the enterprise without immediate attention. Where there are existing dwelling(s) on the enterprise then the need for additional workers to live on the site for the proper functioning of the enterprise must be demonstrated to be essential."

7.5.6   The Practice Guidance (3.9.2) expects this to cover:

> "A description of those aspects of the operation and management of the enterprise which require the presence of a resident worker(s) identifying potential emergency incidents which require a day and night presence
>
> "The identification of any changes in the circumstances of the enterprise which have given rise to the requirement for the presence of a resident worker(s)

"An assessment of the benefits of a transfer of farm management to the younger generation, where relevant."

7.5.7   The assessment is to be based on the character and management of the enterprise, not the personal preferences or circumstances of those involved. The Practice Guidance develops this in paragraph 4.5 and offers a non-exhaustive list of examples in 4.6:

"4.5 Functional need is primarily concerned with the management of risk within the operations of an enterprise such that, without the ready attention of a worker(s), any particular event or combination of events could lead to adverse animal welfare, crop or product quality, or health and safety consequences which might threaten the stability and economic well-being of an enterprise. In all cases, these would be circumstances which could not be properly managed within normal working hours.

"4.6 Examples of the circumstances which might give rise to an essential functional need for a readily available worker are:
– where immediate, regular and often unpredictable care over much of the year is required to safeguard the specific welfare of livestock and offspring in breeding programmes, for example in lambing, calving and foaling conditions, or the more general welfare of animals housed in buildings either permanently or for protracted periods, for example in intensive livestock units, stud and livery stables, or commercial kennels. Rarely occurring (though predictable) events/circumstances or situations of short seasonal 'need' can usually be met through the exemptions offered by Part V of Schedule 2 of the Town and Country Planning (General Permitted Development) Order 1995 (as amended);
– where the productive processes or the quality of crops and products are dependent upon the maintenance and security of controlled environments using automated systems, such as in protected cropping horticulture and intensive livestock units. However, it is often possible to achieve adequate surveillance through remote means such as CCTV and temperature and other environmental sensors;
– where the delivery of specialist services is required outside normal hours and where timeliness of response is important;
– where the lack of 24-hour on-site supervision may prejudice the commercial viability of a business, for example at a large established livery yard.

7.5.8   The Practice Guidance at 4.4 says that where a second dwelling is sought for the transfer of the management of an established farm, there does not have to be the same functional need, it still has to be shown that the purpose cannot be met in another way.

7.5.9   The Time Test – TAN 6 then tests the scale of the labour requirement driven by the Functional Test to demonstrate that there is a substantive need. The time test is applied in three different ways:
– a full-time worker is ordinarily required for a new dwelling :
– the need for at least a half time worker must be shown for a second or further dwelling on an established farm
– rather differently, where the extra farm dwelling is needed for the transfer of the majority control of the farm, the worker must be critical to the successful operation of the farm

7.5.10   TAN 6 states:
"4.9.1 If a functional requirement is established, it will then be necessary to consider the number of workers needed to meet it, for which the scale and nature

of the enterprise will be relevant. Where there is currently no dwelling associated with the rural enterprise the worker for whom there is a functional need for new accommodation must be a full-time worker. With the exception of second dwellings on established farms, it must not relate to a part-time requirement, or a requirement that does not relate to the enterprise. If this is a second (or further) dwelling, all existing dwellings must also be occupied by full-time workers for whom it is essential that they also remain on site for functional reasons, or by workers and their dependents last employed in a rural enterprise. (See exceptions at paragraphs 4.5.1 – 4.5.3)."

7.5.11   The Practice Guidance (3.9.3) expects this to cover:
"An assessment of the labour requirements of the enterprise and a consideration of alternative operational and management strategies available to the enterprise

"An indication of the component parts of the enterprise and the amount of time apportioned to each part"

7.5.12   The Practice Guidance considers that assessing the need for an additional farm dwelling based on the need for a half time worker is hardest to interpret. It sees this as relevant where:
"the existing full-time workforce, probably a single individual, cannot effectively meet all the functional needs of the farm enterprise but the shortfall does not justify a second full-time worker. The introduction of the 0.5 worker would enable the essential functional needs of the enterprise regularly arising over most of the year to be shared and thereby addressed effectively. This would be particularly important where long anti-social hours are involved or it would be unsafe for a single worker to undertake specific tasks. A significant proportion of the additional worker's time needs to be attributed to the essential functional requirements of the agricultural enterprise such as calving or lambing. It would not be appropriate to provide an additional dwelling for a worker merely providing administrative or maintenance support." (Para 4.11)

7.5.13   The assessment of the labour requirement is to be based on standardised calculations using a standard man day of 8 hours with a full time worker providing 275 such days or 2,200 hours, allowing 15-20 per cent on top of the calculation for general maintenance, repairs and management (Practice Guidance, Para 4.15-16).

7.5.14   The Financial Test – TAN 6 then asks that it be shown that the proposal is financially sustainable, taking a five year benchmark. That is though also used to judge a second question as to whether the size and cost of the dwelling is commensurate with the ability of the enterprise to fund it without prejudicing its viability. TAN 6 states:
"4.10.1 The rural enterprise and the activity concerned should be financially sound and should have good prospects of remaining economically sustainable for a reasonable period of time, usually at least 5 years.

"4.10.2 Evidence of actual or potential economic performance will be required. To assess economic sustainability it will be necessary to show the business has a reasonable prospect of providing a market return for all operators for the amount of management and manual labour inputs, including the job for which the rural enterprise dwelling is being sought, for at least five years from the anticipated completion of the proposed development. This should be assessed on the basis of what is a realistic income for the skills of the operator. A financial test is also necessary to assess the size of dwelling which the enterprise can afford to build

67

and maintain. Dwellings which are unusually large in relation to the needs of the enterprise, or unusually expensive to construct in relation to the income it can sustain in the long-term, should not be permitted. It is the requirements of the enterprise rather than of the owner or occupier which are relevant to determining the size of dwelling that is appropriate.

"4.10.3 There may be some cases in which the planning circumstances of the site are such that, if a new permanent dwelling is approved, it will be appropriate for the planning authority to consider making permission subject to a condition removing some of the permitted development rights for development within the curtilage of a dwelling house. For example, proposed extensions could result in a dwelling whose size exceeded what could be justified by the functional requirement, and affect the continued viability of maintaining the property for its intended use given the income which the enterprise can sustain. However, such conditions should only restrict or remove the availability of such specific permitted development rights as are relevant to the circumstances, rather than to be drafted in terms which withdraw all those in a Class."

7.5.15   The Practice Guidance (3.9.4) expects this to cover:
"Details of the actual and/or projected financial performance of the enterprise (accounts, financial statements or business plans) and an assessment of their implications in terms of the proposal."

7.5.16   The Practice Guidance states clearly at 5.2:
"The Rural Enterprise Dwelling policy is concerned with providing support to rural businesses. It relates to commercial entities, and the testing of their financial soundness or prospects derives from the normal economic principles applied to businesses. It is not a policy concerned with unconventional or subsistence enterprises which are the subject of a separate policy approach elsewhere in TAN 6."
That last sentence is taken to be a reference to the One Planet Development policy.

7.5.17   It continues at 5.3:
"5.3 To be viable or sustainable any business enterprise must be:
   • profitable – income must exceed expenditure on a regular basis;
   • feasible – have sufficient funds to support on-going trading operations; and
   • worthwhile – provide a reasonable return on the resources used in it.

"5.4 A business enterprise which is unable to achieve these parameters will not be viable in the long-term. In the short-term, a business might be able to weather difficulties in respect of one of the parameters. However, use of external financial assistance can lead to indebtedness and increased financial liabilities, while persistent absence of reasonable returns undermines the ability of a business to grow and invest in itself. Consequently, while at any time one or more of the parameters might assume a greater importance, ultimately all three are essential to a sustainable enterprise."

7.5.18   The Practice Guidance expects that a business plan will be an important element of an appraisal for new enterprises. No format is prescribed but it should be comprehensive and robust (Para 5.9). It will have added weight where it is endorsed by a third party such as a grant-aiding body or a bank (Para 5.7). The difficulty of future projection is recognised with the suggestion of some testing of sensitivity to risk (Para 5.19).

7.5.19 Existing businesses will need to reveal information about their performance over at least three years (Para 5.11) to show enterprise income, costs of production, net profit and the balance between assets and liabilities (Para 5.14). The profit will be tested for its ability to provide a return to unpaid labour and support the proposed dwelling (Para 5.16). All labour, as identified by the functional test, must be remunerated by either a wage or a return, with statutory minimum wage as the lowest threshold (Para 5.16).

7.5.20 Finance and Building Size – An "indicative build cost" for the dwelling is expected with either the finance for borrowing or a modest return on personal investment to be met from the profit of the enterprise (Para 5.17).

7.5.21 It is understood that in practice some LPAs will not expect the dwelling to be more than 180m^2 and apply a rate of 2.5 per cent.

7.5.22 The size of the dwelling that may be needed (especially for a farmhouse) can conflict with what will be useful for the default use as affordable housing. It may yet be that for some farmhouse applications the accommodation area is distinguished from ancillary space.

7.5.23 The Other Dwelling Test – With the general policy being to restrain new residential development in open countryside, the applicant must show that the need cannot be met, first, by a dwelling already on the business or, second, by converting an existing building.

7.5.24 TAN 6 states:
"4.11.1 Evidence must be provided to demonstrate that there is no other dwelling(s) or buildings suitable for conversion, which are available to meet the need. If there are existing dwelling(s) on the enterprise it needs to be shown why these cannot be used to meet the needs of the enterprise for a resident worker, and why labour or residential arrangements cannot be re-organised to ensure that the existing accommodation meets the needs of the enterprise without the need for a further dwelling.
"4.11.2 In cases where the planning authority is particularly concerned about possible abuse, it may be helpful to investigate the history of the enterprise to establish the recent pattern of use of land and buildings and whether, for example, any dwellings or buildings suitable for conversion to dwellings have recently been sold. Such a sale could constitute evidence of lack of need.

7.5.25 The Practice Guidance (3.9.5) expects the appraisal to cover:
"The identification of existing dwellings associated with the rural enterprise (location, occupancy etc) and of the availability of buildings suitable for conversion
"The availability of alternative existing dwellings in the locality."
That is to be done by reasoned argument or clear robust evidence (Para 6.3). Save where the new dwelling is needed for the transfer of management control:
"The fact that an existing dwelling may be occupied by a person not delivering an essential functional input to the enterprise will not, in itself, be sufficient justification for an additional dwelling." (para 6.4)

7.5.26 When considering a new enterprise this test touches on the suitability of the location for that proposed business itself to show why it could not be located where there is an existing dwelling. (Para 6.8).

7.5.27 Reviewing property websites for dwellings on the market in the necessary area is likely to be part of the process. Many of these may be at prices or rents that are not feasible for the proposition in hand. In the context of possible tenancies, the English case *Embleton* held that the LPA was not unreasonable in accepting that a six month shorthold was so readily terminable that it did not offer a practical alternative to a temporary permission for a caravan for new farm business.

7.5.28 It may be that other recent TAN 6 permissions in the area are themselves presumption that there are no other relevant properties.

7.5.29 Other Planning Requirements Test – Finally, the proposal must satisfy the ordinary requirements of the planning regime:

"4.12.1 Rural enterprise dwellings should satisfy the usual planning requirements in terms of design, sustainability and access. The siting of the proposed dwelling should relate closely to the activities for which there is a need. In most cases this will mean that the new dwelling should be sited in close proximity to existing buildings and in the case of dwellings for agricultural enterprises, should not be isolated from the farmstead or in locations that could encourage farm fragmentation. Local planning authorities should resist planning applications for rural enterprise dwellings that are prominent in the landscape.

"4.12.2 Careful consideration needs to be given to minimising the environmental effects of new rural enterprise dwellings. Opportunities to generate on site power and heat should be explored. Particular attention needs to be given to the avoidance of impacts on ground and surface water, as in most cases, it will not be possible to connect to mains drainage."

7.5.30 The Practice Guidance (3.9.6) expects the appraisal to cover:
"The details of the size, siting, design and projected cost of the proposed dwelling

"An assessment of the suitability of the location of a new rural enterprise in relation to housing requirements".

7.5.31 The scale of the dwelling has already been linked to the financial test. The Practice Guidance advises at Para 7.7 that its size may be relevant to the default affordability occupation by those eligible for affordable housing. The permission is likely to impose a condition as to size.

7.5.32 Conversion of Buildings – The wider policy on residential conversion of commercial buildings is concerned to protect economic opportunities:

"The conversion of buildings which are currently in industrial or commercial use to dwellings may have an adverse impact on the local economy. Where residential conversion is part of a scheme for the re-use of a building or complex of buildings for employment purposes, planning authorities should consider whether to impose a condition requiring the works necessary for the establishment of the enterprise to have been completed before the dwelling is occupied, so as to ensure that the scheme materialises. This may be particularly appropriate in the open countryside. They may also wish to consider whether to impose a condition to tie occupation of the dwelling to the operation of the enterprise, in order to prevent it being sold separately without further application to the authority. Alternatively, they may seek a planning obligation to tie the dwelling to the rest of the building re-use."

7.5.33 However, there is specific guidance on the re-use or conversion of rural buildings: "When assessing planning applications for the re-use or adaptation of a rural building, the primary consideration should be whether the nature and extent of the new use proposed for the building is acceptable in planning terms. It should not normally be necessary to consider whether a building is no longer needed for its present agricultural or other purposes (although in the case of a tenanted agricultural building, the value in planning terms of the existing use should be taken into consideration)." (Para 3.2.1).

However, applications to convert buildings erected under agricultural permitted development rights should be scrutinised for any abuse of the system.

7.6 Rural Enterprise Dwelling Occupancy Conditions

7.6.1 The Welsh Government Circular 16/2014 of October 2014 on the Use of Planning Conditions for Development Management affirms that conditions must meet the six conventional tests from case law, expressed as:

- being necessary
- being relevant to planning
- being relevant to the development
- having considered enforcement
- being precise
- being reasonable.

7.6.2 Its approach in providing model conditions (including one for rural enterprise dwellings) is to offer them as best practice and for use after careful thought, with regard to the six tests and with caution.

7.6.3 The Circular's specific guidance on rural enterprise occupancy conditions at paragraphs 5.85 to 5.91 advises that:

- the development subject to the condition should be sufficiently justified in the first instance
- imposing the condition can draw an artificial and unwarranted distinction between new and existing dwellings. It may:
  - deter the building of new houses for which there may be local demand
  - impose hardship on owners who subsequently need to sell

  and so care should be taken to ensure that an individual's human rights are not harmed.
- however, this is one of few bases for granting permission for new isolated dwellings and so where such a new dwelling is justified by a rural enterprise need that strict control requires that the dwelling remain available for it.

7.6.4 As these permissions are being granted under an exception to general policy against isolated residential development in open countryside, TAN 6 expects them to be made subject to an occupancy condition (Para 4.13.1). It set out a format for that:

"The occupancy of the dwelling shall be restricted to those:

a. solely or mainly working or last working on a rural enterprise in the locality where there is/was a defined functional need; or if it can be demonstrated that there are no such eligible occupiers, to those;

b. who would be eligible for consideration for affordable housing under the local authority's housing policies: or if it can be demonstrated that there are no persons eligible for occupation under either (a) and (b);

c. widows, widowers or civil partners of the above and any resident dependants."

7.6.5 That has now been overtaken by the model recorded below.

7.6.6 Compared with the traditional agricultural occupancy condition, this:
- widens permitted occupation to those in rural enterprises in the locality. Para 4.13.2 suggests it should not be necessary to be more limiting than that and so should allow the dwelling to be available for workers in other rural enterprises in the locality.
- provides the fallback for occupation by those qualifying for affordable housing, potentially making such a condition much harder to lift.

7.6.7 This has since been revised by the Practice Guidance which recognised that:
"8.11 The condition is slightly misleading insofar as it suggests that, if a dwelling no longer meets a rural enterprise need due to the death of the principal worker, the worker's immediate dependant also residing in the dwelling can no longer do so until such time as the absence of a local affordable housing need is demonstrated. This was not the intention of the condition and upon examination in a planning appeal case (Appeal Decision APP/M6825/A/10/2130351) it has been determined that the position of resident dependant relatives is protected."

7.6.8 Thus, since December 2011, the condition should following the wording of the Practice Guidance at Para 8.12:
"The occupancy of the dwelling shall be restricted to:
a) a person solely or mainly working, or last working on a rural enterprise in the locality, or a widow, widower or surviving civil partner of such a person, and to any resident dependants; or, if it can be demonstrated that there are no such eligible occupiers,
b) a person or persons who would be eligible for consideration for affordable housing under the local authority's housing policies, or a widow, widower or surviving civil partner of such a person, and to any resident dependants."

7.6.9 The precise expression of that model condition has again been replaced (with no substantive variation) by the model Occupancy (Rural Enterprise) Condition provided at paragraph 98 of the Appendix to the Welsh Government Circular 16/2014 of October 2014 on the Use of Planning Conditions for Development Management:
"The occupancy of the dwelling shall be restricted to:
a) a person solely or manly working, or last working on a rural enterprise in the locality, or a widow, widower or surviving civil partner of such a person, and to any resident dependants
or if it can demonstrated that there are no such eligible occupiers,
b) a person or persons who would be eligible for consideration for affordable housing under the local authority's housing policies, or a widow, widower or surviving civil partner of such a person, and to any resident dependants".

7.6.10 Neither new draft of the condition refers to there being a functional need. That would be considered in the original grant of permission but is not then entrenched in the permission. Occupiers do not need to demonstrate that functional need beyond simply (last) working in "a rural enterprise in the locality".

7.6.11 Footnotes to the Practice Note's model offer the following points on definitions:
- *"Solely or mainly working"* – "Where someone is predominantly employed in a qualifying rural enterprise".
- *"Last working"* – This "covers the cases of a person who is temporarily unemployed or is no longer able to work due to old age or illness. It may also include a person who is engaged in other part-time or temporary employment

if that person could still be regarded as a rural enterprise worker or a retired rural enterprise worker.

- *"Locality"* – "A rural enterprise worker does not have to live on or adjacent to his/her workplace but may be employed in a rural enterprise at some distance but not so far as to invalidate one of the purposes of the condition which is to preserve a stock of dwellings for the use of the local population."

7.6.12   The Practice Guidance confirms that "locality" is not defined:
"and will vary between types of enterprise and circumstances. Since the occupying worker has to be performing a substantive role in a rural enterprise, long distance commuting is unlikely to be practical or attractive. Distance between a dwelling and work will be determined by considerations such as the nature of the road network, the availability of public transport, and the requirements of a particular enterprise." (Para 8.18)

7.6.13   The purpose of the combined limitation of occupation to rural enterprise workers and those in need of affordable housing (generally as identified in accordance with TAN 2) is made clear:
"The intention is that new rural enterprise dwellings can be continually re-cycled between rural enterprise workers and eligible affordable housing need and their respective dependants. Only in the absence of any eligible occupant within the local area will the release of a dwelling from occupancy control be considered." (Practice Guidance 8.13)

7.6.14   TAN 6 invites LPAs to consider whether such an occupancy condition should be applied to any existing dwellings in the business (Para 4.13.3). The Practice Guidance states that this should not be automatic and instances some examples where this might be done:
- "the need for an additional dwelling arises from an increase in the functional demands of the enterprise whereby two on-site workers are required rather than the one residing in an existing dwelling. In this case it will have been demonstrated that the enterprise needs two dwellings, and it would be inconsistent if the occupancy of the new dwelling was secured and controlled but not that of the existing dwelling."
- "similar circumstances might arise in accommodating the younger generation on existing farming enterprises." (Para 8.22)

7.6.15   The Practice Guidance also considers the use of a s.106 agreement to tie rural dwellings to associated land and buildings.
"However, in considering this method, regard should be had to the normal 'churning' of land assets through their sale and acquisition and the effect of doing so upon the operation of the enterprise. Attention is drawn to paragraph 103 of Circular 35/95 in this regard." (Para 8.23)

7.6.16   Applications to Lift Agricultural Occupancy Conditions – TAN 6 suggests that where there is an application to remove an agricultural occupancy condition or where enforcement action is being taken, the LPA should consider replacing it with the new rural enterprise dwelling condition to ensure that the dwelling is kept available to meet the housing needs of rural workers and local people in need of affordable housing.

7.6.17   Larger questions on this are considered in Chapter 4 above.

7.6.18 Applications to Lift Rural Enterprise Occupancy Conditions – As regards rural enterprise occupation conditions, the Practice Guidance observes that:

> "With the widening of the range of qualifying rural enterprise occupants and the addition of the local affordable housing requirement, the scope for the removal of the new occupancy condition is very much reduced." (Para 8.25)

7.6.19 It suggests that the arguments to be used should be:

> "8.26 … that there is no longer a rural enterprise need for the dwelling or a local affordable housing need in the area. The longstanding mechanism for demonstrating the absence of need has been market testing.

> "8.27 Evidence of effective market testing will be required over a reasonable period, usually at least 12 months. The critical aspects of market testing are that:
> – the availability of a property is advertised in such a manner that compliant purchasers or tenants are likely to be made aware of it; and
> – the price or rent attached to a property reflects the restrictive occupancy requirement."

7.6.20 However, paragraph 5.90 of Circular 16/2014 may appear more liberal in making the need for the condition turn solely on the local need for rural enterprise housing:

> "Where a rural enterprise occupancy condition has been imposed it will not be appropriate to remove it on a subsequent application unless it is shown that the existing need for such dwellings for rural enterprise workers in the locality no longer warrants reserving the house for that purpose."

That suggests that the fallback to affordable housing might be seen as an interim use that is no longer required if there is no further rural enterprise need. That test is however to be assessed on the basis of the locality and not just the business for which the dwelling was originally granted. The Circular does not offer guidance on what is meant by the "locality".

7.6.21 That paragraph further concludes:

> "If planning permission for a dwelling would in all probability be granted without such a condition, this would be a material consideration."

7.6.22 The Practice Guidance offers the Welsh Government's opinions as to the approach to the value of a property with an occupancy condition at 8.28:

> "The value of any property subject to an occupancy restriction will be less than its value on the open market. Traditionally agricultural dwellings have been marketed at prices generally between 70 and 75% of their open market value. With the wider range of compliant rural enterprise workers and local affordability constraints, this will continue to be the case. The valuation of properties will require professional advice and, in the case of affordability criteria, assistance from the local authority."

7.6.23 Perhaps a question that is yet to be tested is whether the fallback to affordable occupation:
> – may reduce the discount because of the greater number of compliant occupiers
> – whether the wider range of rural enterprise users (as well as affordable occupiers) may not influence it because the affordable occupiers may add no further buying power for either purchase or rent.
> – may in some cases increase it, should any hope of lifting the condition be reduced.

All that failing to sell at a particular price shows is that there is at that moment in that area no demand for that property that price.

7.6.24 The legal problems with the suggested marketing process are reviewed in Chapter 4 above. In essence, it may only be lawful if there is a genuine intention to sell while it may be seen as unethical for a professional to market something that is not for sale.

7.6.25 It seems clear that, as is appropriate for affordable housing, the marketing be for rent as well as purchase. The tenancy option may in some circumstances provide an answer where the owner is not willing to sell the dwelling since the use of a shorthold offers an income while retaining flexibility.

7.7 One Planet Development

7.7.1 TAN 6 offers an alternative route at its 4.15 to secure housing in open countryside through One Planet Development that either enhances or does not significantly diminish environmental quality, as an exemplar of Low Impact Development in accordance with the "One Wales: One Planet Sustainable Development Scheme.

7.7.2 These developments could be:
  – single homes, co-operative communities or larger settlements
  – in settlements, adjacent to them or in open countryside.
Where an application is for such a development in open countryside, it should show that, over no more than five years, it would provide the minimum needs of the inhabitants in terms of income, food, energy and waste assimilation if it is to be considered under this policy.

7.7.3 Para 4.16 requires that such an application for an open countryside site must be supported by robust evidence and a management plan:
> "The management plan should set out the objectives of the proposal, timetable for development of the site and timescale for review. It should be used as the basis of a legal agreement relating to the occupation of the site, should planning consent be granted. The management plan should cover the following areas:
> * *Business and Improvement plan* to identify whether there is a need to live on the site and establish the level of the inhabitants' requirements in terms of income, food energy and waste assimilation that can be obtained directly from the site (See paragraph 4.17.1);
> * *Ecological footprint analysis* of the development (See paragraph 4.18.1);
> * *Carbon analysis* of the development (See paragraphs 4.19.1 – 4.19.2);
> * *Biodiversity and landscape assessment* (See paragraph 4.20.1);
> * *Community impact assessment* to identify potential impacts on the host community (both positive and negative) and provide a basis to identify and implement any mitigation measures that may be necessary (See paragraph 4.21.1), and;
> * *Transport assessment and travel plan* to identify the transport needs of the inhabitants and propose sustainable travel solutions. (See paragraph 4.22.1).
Each of these points is considered in subsequent sections of TAN 6.

7.7.4 Circular 16/2014 offers guidance on the use of conditions for this form of development at paragraph 5.97, essentially urging that there be a condition:
> "requiring the use of the site to be carried out in accordance with the management plan supporting the proposed development."
Such a condition is offered at paragraph 99 of the Appendix to the Circular.

7.7.5 Paragraph 100 offers a further model condition requiring the occupiers to submit:
  – annual reports on the previous year's activities, setting our performance against management objectives
  – where performance has fallen short, supplementary reports stating mitigating measures that are to be implemented.

8. RURAL WORKERS' DWELLINGS IN SCOTLAND

8.1   Town and Country Planning Legislation

8.1.1   A comprehensive statutory basis for the administration of development control by local planning authorities within national rules was first laid down as part of the post-war policy reforms in 1947. The present principal statute for Scotland is the Town and Country Planning (Scotland) Act 1997 (TCPA), although this has since been amended in several respects. That post-war framework provided that:

- in general, changes in the use of any land or operations, such as building, to any land are subject to planning control, requiring planning permission
- local authorities were given the powers for the detailed administration of the development control system within a framework of national policies regulated by an appeal system and the courts.
- these Local Planning Authorities (LPAs) were increasingly required to prepare development plans to set out publicly their local policies.

8.1.2   The basic statutory mechanism is that planning permission is required for any development of land (s.28(1)). "Development" is defined at s.26(1) in the same terms as elsewhere in the United Kingdom, as

"the carrying out of building, engineering, mining or other operations in, on, over or under land, or the making of any material change in the use of any buildings or other land".

A critical point is that "development" may be making a change of use or by operations and works.

8.1.3   S.26(4) defines "buildings operations" to include
"(a) demolition of buildings,
(b) rebuilding,
(c) structural alterations of or additions to buildings, and
(d) other operations normally undertaken by a person carrying on business as a builder."

8.1.4   The Act provides its own definition of "land":
"land" includes land covered with water and any building as defined by this section and, in relation to the acquisition of land under Part VIII, includes any interest in land and any servitude or right in or over land;" (s.277)
The definition given for a "building" is
"building" includes any structure or erection, and any part of a building, as so defined, but does not include plant or machinery comprised in a building;" (s.277).

8.1.5   If left at that, the system would pose an impossible level of bureaucracy and process over a complex and changing economy and society, which in practice would lead to wide-scale breach. Therefore, exceptions to that requirement have been made:

- in the statute
- by statutory instruments such as the Use Classes Order (accommodating many changes of use between similar uses) and the General Permitted Development Orders (GPDO) giving general permission, usually subject to conditions, qualifications or notification of the proposal to the LPA
- while guidance has been used to bring varying mixes of certainty or simplicity to the system.

8.1.6 The Exception for Agricultural Use – Reflecting the approach of post-war planning policy, the Act specifically states that the **use** of any land for agriculture (or for forestry) is not to be development:

> "The following operations or uses of land shall not be taken for the purposes of this Act to involve development of the land—
>
> ……
>
> (e) the use of any land for the purposes of agriculture or forestry (including afforestation) and the use for any of those purposes of any building occupied together with land so used;" (s.26(2))

8.1.7 Agriculture itself is defined at s.277 of the TCPA:

> " "agriculture" includes horticulture, fruit growing, seed growing, dairy farming, the breeding and keeping of livestock (including any creature kept for the production of food, wool, skins or fur, or for the purpose of its use in the farming of land), the use of land as grazing land, meadow land, osier land, market gardens and nursery grounds, and the use of land for woodlands where that use is ancillary to the farming of land for other agricultural purposes, and "agricultural" shall be construed accordingly;"

These are the same terms as used for planning legislation in England and Wales and close to those used for tenancy legislation and have been the subject of judicial decisions, especially in the context of equestrian uses. Forestry is not defined in the Act. The important point is that this concerns the use of land, not any construction works.

8.2 Scottish Planning Policy

8.2.1 National Policy – Planning policy at a national level is currently delivered through two major documents:

- the National Planning Framework setting out the Scottish Government's strategy for Scotland's long-term spatial development. The second NPF was issued in 2009 and work is underway on the third edition. In looking ahead to 2030 it intends to "support sustainable growth in the rural economy".
- Scottish Planning Policy (SPP) setting out Scottish Government policy on nationally important land use planning matters. SPP 2014 opens its section on Purposes at paragraph (i) saying:

  "The purpose of the SPP is to set out national planning policies which reflect Scottish Ministers' priorities for operation of the planning system and for the development and use of land. The SPP promotes consistency in the application of policy across Scotland whilst allowing sufficient flexibility to reflect local circumstances. It directly relates to:
  - the preparation of development plans;
  - the design of development, from initial concept through to delivery; and
  - the determination of planning applications and appeals."

These documents are supported by Government Circulars and Planning Advice Notes (PANs).

8.2.2 Local Development Plans – The TCPA requires local authorities to create development plans to manage development control (s.11(1)). The local plans must go through a process of consultation and independent examination before being submitted to Ministers. S.37(2) TCPA requires that in dealing with an application for planning permission:

> "the authority shall have regard to the provisions of the development plan, so far as material to the application, and to any other material considerations."

8.2.3   Scottish Planning Policy – Scottish Planning Policy 2010 consolidated the previous range of specific policy statements into a single, shorter statement on land use policies. In doing that, it replaced the previous SPP15, Planning for Rural Development. It contained:

- an overview of the key components and overall aims and principles of the planning system.
- overall policies on sustainable economic growth, community engagement and sustainable development.
- specific policies on: economic development, town centres and retailing, housing, rural development, coastal planning, fish farming, historic environment, landscape and natural heritage, open space and physical activity, green belts, transport, renewable energy, flooding and drainage, waste management, minerals, on-shore oil and gas, surface coal mining and communications infrastructure.

and set out what the Scottish Government intends the planning system to achieve, including the creation of "high quality sustainable places and increased sustainable economic growth".

8.2.4   A review commenced in 2012 with a draft published in April 2013 and the final document published in June 2014. This process has been run in conjunction with the review of the National Planning Framework.

8.2.5   SPP 2010 – Rural Housing – The general policy towards housing was set out at paragraph 84 in the section on the Location and Design of New Development:

"The majority of housing land requirements will be met within or adjacent to existing settlements and this approach will help to minimise servicing costs and sustain local schools, shops and services. Authorities should also set out the circumstances in which new housing outwith settlements may be appropriate, particularly in rural areas. Development plans should promote the development of rural communities and aim to support and sustain fragile and dispersed communities through appropriate housing development. In areas where there is a large demand for holiday or second homes, planning authorities should respond to this demand through the housing land allocation. Policy on housing in rural areas is also covered in the rural development section of this SPP."

8.2.6   Rural housing was further considered in the section on Rural Development with this statement in Paragraph 94:

"Development plans should support more opportunities for small scale housing development in all rural areas, including new clusters and groups, extensions to existing clusters and groups, replacement housing, plots on which to build individually designed houses, holiday homes and new build or conversion housing which is linked to rural businesses or would support the formation of new businesses by providing funding.

8.2.7   That provided a tolerance at national level for individual plots and using either new build or conversion to provide housing to support existing rural businesses or the formation of new ones.

8.2.8   The paragraph continued to enlarge on that last theme:

"Opportunities to replace rundown housing and steadings, and to provide limited new housing along with converted rehabilitated buildings, should be supported where the new development is designed to fit in the landscape setting and will result a cohesive grouping. Modernisation and steading conversion should not be constrained within the original footprint or height limit unless there are compelling design or conservation reasons for doing so."

8.2.9 The case was further put in paragraph 95:
"In less populated areas, small scale housing and other development which supports diversification and other opportunities for sustainable economic growth whilst respecting and protecting the natural and cultural heritage should be supported in a range of locations. In these areas, new housing outwith existing settlements may have a part to play in economic regeneration and environmental renewal. All new development should respond to the specific local character of the location, fit in the landscape and seek to achieve high design and environmental standards, particularly in relation to energy efficiency. Planning authorities should apply proportionate standards to access roads to enable small developments to remain viable."

8.2.10 Paragraph 97 allowed that, even on prime agricultural land:
"Small scale development directly linked to rural businesses, including housing, may also be permitted."

8.2.11 Scottish Planning Policy 2014 – After review, a new policy statement was issued in June 2014. Under the heading of "Promoting Rural Development" it proposed general approaches to rural development varying with the remoteness of the rural area to apply the National Planning Framework 3's vision of "vibrant rural, coastal and island areas, with growing, sustainable communities supported by new opportunities for employment and education."

8.2.12 At paragraph 75 on policy principles, it advises that:
"The planning system should:
• in all rural and island areas promote a pattern of development that is appropriate to the character of the particular rural area and the challenges it faces;
• encourage rural development that supports prosperous and sustainable communities and businesses whilst protecting and enhancing environmental quality; and
• support an integrated approach to coastal planning.

8.2.13 SPP 2014 expects that development plans should have a spatial strategy that, among other things:
"promotes economic activity and diversification, including, where appropriate, sustainable development linked to tourism and leisure, forestry, farm and croft diversification and aquaculture, nature conservation, and renewable energy developments, while ensuring that the distinctive character of the area, the service function of small towns and natural and cultural heritage are protected and enhanced" (paragraph 79).

8.2.14 Paragraph 81 advises that
"In more accessible or pressured rural areas, where there is a danger of unsustainable growth in long-distance car-based commuting or suburbanisation of the countryside, a more restrictive approach to new housing development is appropriate, and plans and decision-making should generally:
• guide most new development to locations within or adjacent to settlements; and
• set out the circumstances in which new housing outwith settlements may be appropriate, avoiding use of occupancy restrictions".

8.2.15 Paragraph 83 considers more remote rural areas:
"... where new development can often help to sustain fragile communities, plans and decision-making should generally:
- encourage sustainable development that will provide employment;
- support and sustain fragile and dispersed communities through provision for appropriate development, especially housing and community-owned energy;
- include provision for small-scale housing and other development which supports sustainable economic growth in a range of locations, taking account of environmental protection policies and addressing issues of location, access, siting, design and environmental impact;
- where appropriate, allow the construction of single houses outwith settlements provided they are well sited and designed to fit with local landscape character, taking account of landscape protection and other plan policies;
- not impose occupancy restrictions on housing".

8.2.16 The key points here appear to be that:
- small scale housing (including new build or conversion linked to rural business) is to be allowed to support economic growth subject to design and impact
- single houses outside settlements are anyway to be allowed subject to siting and design
- no occupancy conditions are to be imposed.

A footnote defines "small scale housing" as "including clusters and groups; extensions to existing clusters and groups; replacement housing; plots for self build; holiday homes; new build or conversion linked to rural business."

8.2.17 Overall, these policies make no reference to housing for agricultural or forestry uses, being based generally on rural businesses.

8.2.18 **Housing for Retiring Tenant Farmers** – The Scottish Government's Chief Planner wrote to Heads of Planning in November 2009 to draw to their attention a recommendation of the Tenant Farming Forum that easing the retirement housing of a tenant famer could open opportunities for new entrants, assisting the rural economy. Asking them
"to consider the need to plan positively to meet the housing needs of retiring tenant farmers",
he advised that
"The ability of landlords of such farms to construct a house on their land to provide accommodation for retiring tenants, where the incomer to the new tenancy takes up residency in the existing property on the agricultural holding, is seen as key in this context. ... Another option, provided land was available, would be to make provision for housing on other land nearby, perhaps in or close to a settlement. There might also be opportunities for the conversion of existing dwellings."

8.3 Planning Conditions

8.3.1 Conditions are frequently attached to planning consents, including those for agricultural dwellings.

8.3.2 Planning conditions may only be imposed if they meet certain statutory requirements and may be subject to appeal if they do not meet non-statutory tests. Statutory authority for the principle of applying a condition to a planning consent is given by s.37(1) TCPA:
"Where an application is made to a planning authority for planning permission—
(a) subject to sections 58 and 59, they may grant planning permission, either unconditionally or subject to such conditions as they think fit, or
(b) they may refuse planning permission."

The matter of conditions is then expanded on by s.41(1):

"(1) Without prejudice to the generality of section 37(1) to (3), conditions may be imposed on the grant of planning permission under that section—

(a) for regulating the development or use of any land under the control of the applicant (whether or not it is land in respect of which the application was made) or requiring the carrying out of works on any such land, so far as appears to the planning authority to be expedient for the purposes of or in connection with the development authorised by the permission;

(b) for requiring the removal of any buildings or works authorised by the permission, or the discontinuance of any use of land so authorised, at the end of a specified period, and the carrying out of any works required for the reinstatement of land at the end of that period."

8.3.3   The approach to the use of planning conditions was set out at paragraph 26 of Scottish Planning Policy 2010:

"Conditions imposed on the grant of planning permission can enable development proposals to proceed where it would otherwise have been necessary to withhold planning permission. While the power to impose conditions is wide, it must be exercised in a manner which is fair, reasonable and practicable and the conditions imposed must accord with the established tests set out in Circular 4/1998 *The Use of Conditions in Planning Permissions*."

Scottish Planning Policy 2014 only refers to imposing them where they are necessary (paragraph 4).

8.3.4   Circular 4/1998, which still appears to be current, sets out guidance on the conventional six tests from case law of the need for a condition, relevance to planning, relevance to the development to be permitted, ability to enforce, precision and reasonableness.

8.3.5   Occupancy Conditions – Paragraphs 100 to 102 of Circular 4/1998 specifically consider agricultural and forestry occupancy conditions:

"100. In many parts of Scotland planning policies impose strict controls on new residential development in the open countryside. There may, however, be circumstances where permission is granted to allow a house to be built to accommodate a worker engaged in *bona fide* agricultural or forestry employment on a site where residential development would not normally be permitted. In these circumstances, it will often be necessary to impose an agricultural or forestry worker occupancy condition.

"101. Planning authorities will wish to take care to frame agricultural occupancy conditions in such a way as to ensure that their purpose is clear. In particular, they will wish to ensure that the condition does not have the effect of preventing future occupation by retired agricultural workers or the dependants of the agricultural occupant.

"102. Where an agricultural occupancy condition has been imposed, it will not be appropriate to remove it on a subsequent application unless it is shown that circumstances have materially changed and that the agricultural need which justified the approval of the house in the first instance no longer exists."

8.3.6   The Addendum to the Circular on Model Planning Conditions issued in March 1999 offered (paragraph C6(a)) a form of words for a condition for agricultural and forestry occupancy conditions:

"Occupation of the dwelling shall be limited to a person solely or mainly employed, or last employed in the locality in [*specify*] or to a widow or widower of such a person and to any dependants."

8.3.7 New Guidance – A letter issued by the Scottish Government's Director and Chief Planner to the local authority Heads of Planning on 4th November 2011 stated in bold type that:

"The Scottish Government believes that occupancy restrictions are rarely appropriate and so should generally be avoided".

It affirmed that "Scottish Planning Policy ... does not promote the use of occupancy restrictions." Where the council is satisfied that there is an adequate land management or business case "it should not be necessary to use formal mechanisms to restrict occupancy". A more restrictive approach might be justified in areas at risk of suburbanisation or to contain long distance commuting. This approach puts the onus on the planning authority to justify using a condition. That general preference not to impose occupancy conditions is affirmed by Scottish Planning Policy 2014 as reviewed in section 8.2 above.

8.3.8   It may be noted that some councils such as Stirling, feeling under development pressure, responded to the Chief Planner's letter by looking to use conditions rather than agreements.

8.3.9   Much of the text in Chapter 4 above on lifting conditions will be relevant for consideration in Scotland, making appropriate allowances for legislation and circumstances. In that, the Consumer Protection from Unfair Trading Regulations 2008 apply also in Scotland and so pose the same issues for marketing exercises.

8.4   Section 75 Agreements and Obligations
8.4.1   Planning obligations made under s.75 of the TCPA 1997 are legally binding commitments by the developer to the local authority and the developer which aim to make the impact of a development acceptable. While a planning condition can be challenged or lifted, an agreement can only be varied by agreement.

8.4.2   The approach to the use of planning agreements was set out at paragraph 27 of Scottish Planning Policy 2010:

"Planning agreements can be used to overcome obstacles to the grant of planning permission but they should not be used to obtain a benefit which is unrelated to the nature or scale of the proposed development. Planning authorities should use the development plan and supplementary guidance to set out their approach to planning agreements and should not seek to introduce agreements late in the development management process. Planning agreements should only be used where the obligation cannot be secured by condition or by other means. More information on planning agreements is provided in Circular 1/2010 *Planning Agreements*."

Scottish Planning Policy 2014 simply refers to using obligations where necessary but, in the meantime, policy has been set out in Circular 3/2012, Planning Obligations and Good Neighbour Agreements, which replaced Circular 1/2010.

8.4.3   Circular 3/2012 seeks obligations that meet five tests of:
  – necessity
  – planning purpose
  – relationship to proposed development
  – scale and kind
  – reasonableness.

8.4.4   A planning authority may also seek to use an agreement under s.75 (previously s.50) to link the new dwelling to the holding so that it cannot be sold away separately. Councils have also used them to regulate occupation, seeing them as less problematic than conditions. It is now possible that the owner of the land who originally entered into such a planning agreement will remain liable for implementing its terms even after selling the affected land.

8.4.5   In an agricultural context, a s.75 agreement might be used to tie the ownership of the dwelling to the ownership of the farmland that supported its application. While the LPA can feel that helps protect the policy purpose of the permission given and limit its fears of subsequent abuse, that can lead to practical issues where some land needs to be sold or the business restructures.

8.4.6   The letter written by the Scottish Government's Director and Chief Planner to the local authority Heads of Planning on 4th November 2011 read as though its advice against occupancy conditions applied equally to planning agreement and obligations:
> "In determining an application for a new house in the countryside, it may be appropriate for the planning authority to consider the need for a house in that location, especially where there is the potential for adverse impacts. In these circumstances, it is reasonable for decision-makers to weigh the justification for the house against its impact, for example on road safety, landscape quality or natural heritage, and in such circumstances it may be appropriate for applicants to be asked to make a land management or other business case. Where the authority is satisfied that an adequate case has been made, it should not be necessary to use formal mechanisms to restrict occupancy."

8.4.7   That view is confirmed by Circular 3/2012 at its paragraph 50 and 51
> "Such restrictions have historically been used particularly in respect of housing in rural areas. Imposing restrictions on use are rarely appropriate and so should generally be avoided. They can be intrusive, resource-intensive, difficult to monitor and enforce and can introduce unnecessary burdens or constraints. In determining an application, it may be appropriate for the planning authority to consider the need for the development in that location, especially where there is the potential for adverse impacts. In these circumstances, it is reasonable for decision-makers to weigh the justification against the potential impacts, for example on road safety, landscape quality or natural heritage, and in such circumstances it may be appropriate for applicants to be asked to make a land management or other business case.

> "Where the authority is satisfied that an adequate case has been made, it should not be necessary to use a planning obligation as a formal mechanism to restrict occupancy or use."

8.4.8   In Scotland, an appeal against a refusal by the LPA to remove or modify an obligation or agreement can be made to Scottish ministers (the Directorate for Planning and Environmental Appeals). The Scottish Government's Chief Planner wrote to Heads of Planning in July 2011 to confirm that, while there was legal debate, the new procedures for such applications applied to all agreements and obligations under s.75. Unlike England and Wales, there is no initial five year bar on such appeals.

9. RURAL WORKERS DWELLINGS IN NORTHERN IRELAND

9.1 Introduction

9.1.1 The management of development control in Northern Ireland is going through a process of change at the time of writing putting an English style system in place with general overall guidance to new Councils who are in future to determine policy and decisions within that. This will be a marked shift from a more centralised system that has held for several decades.

9.1.2 Three departments handle planning:
- the Department of Regional Development is responsible for strategic planning and implementation of the Regional Development Strategy
- the Department of the Environment handles development control including the development of Area Plans
- the Department of Social Development covering development initiatives and action plans outside the strategic frameworks.

For the purposes of this text, development control currently lies with Town and Country Planning Service, an agency of the Department of the Environment with its six divisional planning offices. The 26 current district councils have a consultative role.

9.2 Town and Country Planning Legislation

9.2.1 The present principal statute for Northern Ireland is the Planning Act (Northern Ireland) 2011. The basic statutory mechanism is that planning permission is required for any development of land (s.24(1)). "Development" is defined at s.23(1) in the same terms as elsewhere in the United Kingdom, as

"the carrying out of building, engineering, mining or other operations in, on, over or under land, or the making of any material change in the use of any buildings or other land".

A critical point is that is that "development" may be making a change of use or by operations and works.

9.2.2 S.23(2) defines "building operations" to include
"(a) demolition of buildings;
(b) rebuilding;
(c) structural alteration of or addition to buildings; and
(d) other operations normally undertaken by a person carrying on business as a builder."

9.2.3 The Act does not provide a definition of "land" and so it is taken the definition in s.45(1) of the Interpretation Act (Northern Ireland) 1954 applies:
"References relating to land.
(1) In any enactment passed after the commencement of this Act the expression—
(a) "land" shall include—
    (i) messuages, tenements and hereditaments of any tenure;
    (ii) land covered by water;
    (iii) any estate in land or water; and
    (iv) houses or other buildings or structures whatsoever."

9.2.4 The Act does give a definition for a "building":
"building" includes any structure or erection, and any part of a building, as so defined, but does not include plant or machinery comprised in a building;" (s.250).
following the wording used elsewhere in the United Kingdom.

9.2.5   If left at that, the system would pose an impossible level of bureaucracy and process over a complex and changing economy and society, which in practice would lead to wide-scale breach. Therefore, exceptions to that requirement have been made:

- in the statute
- by statutory instruments such as:
  - the Use Classes Order, accommodating many changes of use between similar uses – most recently the Planning (Use Classes) Order (Northern Ireland) 2004)
  - the Planning (General Development) Order (Northern Ireland) 1993 (the "GDO") as amended giving general permission for specified types of development, such as for some agricultural buildings, usually subject to conditions, qualifications or notification of the proposal to the LPA

while guidance has been used to bring varying mixes of certainty or simplicity to the system.

9.2.6   The Exception for Agricultural Use – Reflecting the approach of post-war planning policy, the Act specifically states that the **use** of any land for agriculture (or for forestry) is not to be development:

"The following operations or uses of land shall not be taken for the purposes of this Act to involve development of the land—

......

(d) the use of any land for the purposes of agriculture or forestry and the use for any of those purposes of any building occupied together with land so used;" (s.23(3)).

That is essentially the same exemption as elsewhere in the United Kingdom but omits the express inclusion of "afforestation" in "forestry".

9.2.7   Agriculture itself is defined at s.250 of the Planning Act:

" "agriculture" includes horticulture, fruit growing, seed growing, dairy farming and livestock breeding and keeping, the use of land as grazing lands, meadow land, market gardens and nursery grounds, and the use of land for woodlands where that use is ancillary to the farming of land for other agricultural purposes;"

That uses substantially the same terms as the definitions used in England and Wales and in Scotland though:

- it omits the inclusion within livestock of "(including any creature kept for the production of food, wool, skins or fur, or for the purpose of its use in the farming of land)"
- grazing lands are plural here
- there is no mention of osier land

but it is probable that, save in very exceptional cases nothing turns on these points and so wider judicial decisions will generally be relevant. The important point is that this concerns the use of land, not any construction works.

9.2.8   Forestry is not defined in the Act.

9.3   Development Control Policy Framework

9.3.1   S.5 of the Planning Act (Northern Ireland) 2011 sets "the objective of furthering sustainable development" for all involved in development control policy who are to take account of policies and guidance issued by the Office of the First Minister and deputy First Minister, the Departments of the Environment and for Regional Development as well as any matters which appear to that person to be relevant.

9.3.2 There are three levels of document:
- **Regional Development Strategy** – The present document, issued in 2012, offers a framework for planning until 2035. All planning policies and plans are to be "in general conformity" with the Strategy.
- **Planning Policy Statements (PPS)** – These set out the Department's planning policies for the whole of Northern Ireland and so the main planning considerations that the Department takes into account in assessing planning applications and may be relevant to the preparation of development plans.
- **Development Plans** – These may be area plans, local plans or subject plans, applying the Department's policies at a local level and to be taken into account in deciding applications. As well as allocating land, they outline the local balance to be struck between development and protection of the environment in each area.

9.4 Use of Planning Conditions and Planning Agreements

9.4.1 PPS1 sets out policy on the use of both conditions and planning agreements.

9.4.2 Planning Conditions – Paragraph 56 states that:
"… the Department will only impose conditions that, in its opinion, are necessary, relevant to planning, relevant to the development being permitted, precise, enforceable and reasonable in all other respects. One key test of whether a particular condition is necessary is if planning permission would have been refused if the condition were not imposed. Otherwise, such a condition would need special and precise justification.

9.4.3 With comments more closely related to occupancy conditions, paragraph 57 says: "Unless otherwise specified, a planning permission relates to land rather than those persons who own or occupy it. The Department considers that it is seldom desirable to provide for any other arrangement. However, the personal or domestic circumstances of an applicant, or the difficulties encountered by a business that is of value to the local community, may, exceptionally be material to the consideration of a planning application. While such arguments will seldom outweigh general planning policy considerations, in exceptional circumstances, the Department may grant planning permission subject to a condition that it is personal to the applicant.

9.4.4 Planning Agreements – Article 40 of the Planning (Northern Ireland) Order 1991 as amended by Article 23 of the Planning (Amendment) (Northern Ireland) Order 2003 allows anyone with an interest in the land to enter into an agreement with the Department as to the use of the land. After five years, an application may be made to the Department to modify or discharge the agreement and refusal can be referred to the Planning Appeals Commission.

9.4.5 PPS1 sets out policy on the use of agreements at paragraphs 62 to 66, including at paragraphs 62 to 64:
"… If there is a choice between imposing planning conditions and entering into a planning agreement, the Department will normally opt for conditions since they are simpler to administer and are subject to appeal. … Before entering into a planning agreement, the Department will wish to be satisfied that it provides an acceptable means of overcoming the particular obstacles to development. … The Department will seek planning agreements only where the benefit sought is related to the development and necessary to the grant of permission. Unacceptable development will not be permitted because of unrelated benefits

offered by the applicant nor will acceptable development be refused permission simply because the applicant is unable or unwilling to offer such unrelated benefits. Planning agreements can apply to land, roads or buildings other than those covered by the planning permission provided there is a direct relationship between the two. Agreements will not be sought where this connection does not exist or is too remote to be considered reasonable."

9.4.6   At paragraph 65 it advises that
"The Department regards it as reasonable to seek planning agreements where what is required:
- is needed to enable the development to go ahead; or
- will contribute to meeting the cost of providing necessary facilities in the near future; or
- is otherwise so directly related to the proposed development and to the use of the land after its completion, that the development ought not to be permitted without it; or
- is designed to secure an acceptable balance of uses; or
- is designed to secure the implementation of development plan policies in respect of a particular area or type of development; or
- is intended to offset the loss of or impact on any amenity or resource present on the site prior to development."

9.5   Planning Policy and Rural Housing
9.5.1   The Regional Development Strategy appears to say nothing directly on rural workers' housing with commentary rather on the rural economy. Its Rural Area chapter states:
"3.96 To sustain rural communities, new development and employment opportunities which respect local, social and environmental circumstances are required. This means facilitating the development of rural industries, businesses and enterprises in appropriate locations, and ensuring they are integrated appropriately within the settlement or rural landscape. The expansion of rural tourism and associated development that is both sustainable and environmentally sensitive should be encouraged."
The associated policy is then:
"SFG13: Sustain rural communities living in smaller settlements and the open Countryside"

9.5.2   Among the points noted in 3.101 is
"• **Facilitate the development of rural industries, businesses and enterprises in appropriate locations.** Farming plays a major part in sustaining rural community networks, as employers, consumers and producers. Forestry and fishing also contribute to communities, in employment and commercial terms, as well as in terms of recreation opportunities. Other industries such as tourism and renewable energy can provide further jobs and opportunities in rural areas as long they are integrated appropriately within the settlement or rural landscape.
"• **Encourage sustainable and sensitive development.** The expansion of rural tourism and development which is both sustainable and sensitive to the environment should be encouraged. This includes the ability of settlements and landscapes to absorb development."

9.5.3   The Housing Evaluation Framework's Urban and Rural Character Test (Table 3.2) wishes development to maintain a "sense of place". Paragraph 3.98 recognises the distinctive pattern of rural settlement in Northern Ireland and 3.99 notes the particular issue of Rathlin Island as the province's only inhabited offshore island (which has its own separate Action Plan).

9.5.4   The issues of rural workers' housing are left for more specific documents – at regional level, the PPSs.

9.6   PPS21: Sustainable Development in the Countryside

9.6.1   Northern Ireland's planning policy for dwellings in the countryside is set out in Planning Policy Statement PPS21, Sustainable Development in the Countryside, which was published in 2010. It is due to be replaced by a new Strategic Planning Policy as part of the reform of the planning system in Northern Ireland (see section 9.7 below).

9.6.2   Its Preamble states that it applies to all
"land lying outside of settlement limits as identified in development plans"
and takes precedence over a wide range of previous policies.

9.6.3   Certain areas such as the High Mournes are to be identified as Special Countryside Areas:
"wherein the quality of the landscape and unique amenity value is such that development should only be permitted in exceptional circumstances." (Para 4.4)

9.6.4   Other areas may be identified as "Dispersed Rural Communities", effectively recognised as settlements rather than as open country.

9.6.5   The overall policy is set out in CTY1, Development in the Countryside, of which the parts most relevant to rural workers' housing are:
"There are a range of types of development which in principle are considered to be acceptable in the countryside and that will contribute to the aims of sustainable development. Details of these are set out below.

"Other types of development will only be permitted where there are overriding reasons why that development is essential and could not be located in a settlement, or it is otherwise allocated for development in a development plan.

"All proposals for development in the countryside must be sited and designed to integrate sympathetically with their surroundings and to meet other planning and environmental considerations including those for drainage, access and road safety. Access arrangements must be in accordance with the Department's published guidance.

"Where a Special Countryside Area (SCA) is designated in a development plan, no development will be permitted unless it complies with the specific policy provisions of the relevant plan.

"Housing Development
"Planning permission will be granted for an individual dwelling house in the countryside in the following cases:
– a dwelling sited within an existing cluster of buildings in accordance with Policy CTY 2a;
– a replacement dwelling in accordance with Policy CTY 3;

- a dwelling based on special personal or domestic circumstances in accordance with Policy CTY 6;
- a dwelling to meet the essential needs of a non-agricultural business enterprise in accordance with Policy CTY 7;
- the development of a small gap site within an otherwise substantial and continuously built up frontage in accordance with Policy CTY 8; or
- a dwelling on a farm in accordance with Policy CTY 10.

"Planning permission will also be granted in the countryside for:
- a small group of houses in a designated Dispersed Rural Community in accordance with Policy CTY 2;
- the conversion of a non-residential building to a dwelling(s) in accordance with Policy CTY 4;
- the provision of social and affordable housing in accordance with Policy CTY 5;
- a residential caravan or mobile home in accordance with Policy CTY 9;
- the conversion of a listed building to residential accommodation in accordance with the policies of PPS 6;
- …"

9.6.6   This is represented as a tightening of policy following concern that accelerating development pressure, especially for single dwellings, is now an unsustainable threat to the environment. Concern to ensure economic development opportunities in the countryside leads to particular recognition of:
- agriculture and agricultural diversification to maintain or increase farm income and employment. "The planning system will therefore continue to sympathetically view appropriate farm diversification schemes." (Para 5.9)
- "tourism growth, particularly through the sympathetic conversion or re-use of existing buildings in the countryside. Exceptionally, new build accommodation may also be acceptable" (Para 5.10).
- "appropriate industrial and commercial enterprises, including minerals development and necessary infrastructure will be facilitated" (Para 5.11).

9.6.7   Dwellings for Non-Agricultural Business Enterprises – The main policy specifically for housing for rural workers in established businesses is Policy CTY7 which provides that
"Planning permission will be granted for a dwelling house in connection with an established non-agricultural business enterprise where a site specific need can be clearly demonstrated that makes it essential for one of the firm's employees to live at the site of their work.

"Where such a need is accepted the dwelling house will need to be located beside, or within, the boundaries of the business enterprise and integrate with the buildings on the site.

"Planning permission granted under this policy will be subject to a condition restricting occupation of the dwelling for the use of the business."

9.6.8   Key points in the commentary include:
- the need to provide sufficient information to show that there is a site specific need which makes it essential for one of the firm's employees to live at the site of their work.
- where a business has been operating satisfactorily without residential accommodation, it will be expected to demonstrate why accommodation is

now considered necessary in order to enable the enterprise to function properly.

– any need to provide improved security from theft and/or vandalism by having someone living on the site is unlikely on its own to warrant the grant of planning permission.

9.6.9   The prospect of a limited occupancy condition will need to be considered.

9.6.10   Dwellings on Farms or Commercial Horse Businesses – Policy CTY10 sets out the policy for dwellings on farms offering a generally tolerant framework, with a concluding provision for equine businesses.

"Planning permission will be granted for a dwelling house on a farm where all of the following criteria can be met:

(a) the farm business is currently active and has been established for at least 6 years;

(b) no dwellings or development opportunities out-with settlement limits have been sold off from the farm holding within 10 years of the date of the application. This provision will only apply from 25 November 2008; and

(c) the new building is visually linked or sited to cluster with an established group of buildings on the farm and where practicable, access to the dwelling should be obtained from an existing lane. Exceptionally, consideration may be given to an alternative site elsewhere on the farm, provided there are no other sites available at another group of buildings on the farm or out-farm, and where there are either:

– demonstrable health and safety reasons; or

– verifiable plans to expand the farm business at the existing building group(s).

"In such circumstances the proposed site must also meet the requirements of CTY 13(a-f), CTY 14 and CTY 16.

"Planning permission granted under this policy will only be forthcoming once every 10 years.

"A proposal for a dwelling by those involved in the keeping and breeding of horses for commercial purposes will also be assessed under the criteria set out in this policy."

9.6.11   The policies referred to are essentially about that "sense of place":

– CTY 13 – Integration and Design of Buildings in the Countryside;

– CTY 14 – Rural Character

– CTY 16 – The Setting of Settlements

9.6.12   Some key points in the commentary on this policy are

– the existing farming business is both established and active. The applicant will need to provide the farm's DARD business ID number and other evidence to prove active farming over the required period. The definition of "agricultural activity" here refers to

"the production, rearing or growing of agricultural products including harvesting, milking, breeding animals and keeping animals for farming purposes, or maintaining the land in good agricultural and environmental condition".

This is drawn from that for the Single Payment Scheme.

– qualifying equine businesses include horse breeding and training, the operating of livery yards, trekking centres and riding schools. Applicants will have to provide sufficient information to demonstrate a level of involvement commensurate with commercial activity for 6 years, including:
  – a statement of commercial rateable history for the business;
  – copies of appropriate insurances;
  – copies of horse passports (if applicable); and
any other information considered relevant to the particular case.
– permission will not be granted for a dwelling under this policy if the business:
  – has recently disposed of a development opportunity from the farm (including a transfer to a family member) such as a replacement dwelling or other building capable of conversion
  – has been artificially divided solely for the purpose of obtaining planning permission.
– the dwellings should be positioned sensitively with the farm's buildings. It will not be acceptable to position a new dwelling with buildings which are on a neighbouring farm holding.
– where a site away from the farm buildings is proposed, the applicant will need to submit good supporting evidence as appropriate:
  – on health and safety from an authority such as the Health and Safety Executive or Environmental Health Department of the local Council to justify the siting. (Note – Subsequent advice from the Department says applicants are not to ask these bodies before making the planning application.)
  – on future business expansion which may include valid planning permissions, building control approvals or contractual obligations to supply farm produce.

9.6.13 Other Policies for Housing – PPS 21 includes several other policies for residential development in the countryside:

- CTY4: **The Conversion and Re-use of Existing Buildings** – Permission will be granted for the sympathetic conversion of a suitable building to a variety of uses, including use as a single dwelling. Proposals are to be of a "high design quality" and must meet certain criteria, including a requirement that "the reuse or conversion would not unduly affect the amenities of nearby residents or adversely affect the continued agricultural use of adjoining land or buildings".
- CTY3: **Replacement Dwellings** – Planning permission will be granted for a replacement dwelling where the building to be replaced exhibits the essential characteristics of a dwelling and as a minimum all external structural walls are substantially intact.
- CTY6: **Personal and Domestic Circumstances** – Permission for a new dwelling will be granted to meet the long term needs of the applicant, where there are compelling, and site specific reasons for this related to the applicant's personal or domestic circumstances. The permission will include a personal occupation condition. The example quoted in the supporting text is that of a young adult who needs close personal care but requires independent living.

9.6.14 Conditions – Only polices CTY 6 (Personal Circumstances) and CTY 7 (Established Rural Businesses) make provision for occupation conditions and these may be very limiting. CTY 10 makes no provision for an occupancy condition (though an equivalent user condition is to be applied under CTY12 to permissions for farm buildings outside the GDO) but its presumption against further permissions for 10 years may have some of the same effect.

9.6.15   The commentary on CTY 13 notes two potential subjects of conditions:
– the extent of the curtilage of any new dwelling, to limit the size of gardens in open country
– in the context of access arrangements, the removal of permitted development rights in respect of boundary features.

9.6.16   In the context of the problems with mortgage finance posed by occupancy conditions under CTY6, the July 2013 ministerial statement by Alex Attwood on PPS 21 said:

"Recently, I drafted and issued a new 'letter of comfort' which I have advised the Council for Mortgage Lenders should conclude the problems the CML or its members were creating around this issue. "

9.6.17   New Businesses – PPS 21 is addressed essentially to established businesses, including farms and horse businesses that have been active for at least six years, and does not consider new businesses. It may be that CTY9, Residential Caravans and Mobile Homes (with its emphasis on temporary permissions) would be used in such cases where warranted.

9.7   Planning Reform
9.7.1   The planning system in Northern Ireland is undergoing major reform, including the transfer of responsibility for many planning functions from the Department of the Environment to eleven newly created district councils with effect from April 2015 which are to prepare their own development plans. S.5 of the Planning Act (Northern Ireland) 2011 requires that to be done:
"(1) … with the objective of furthering sustainable development.
(2)   For the purposes of subsection (1) the person must take account of —
(a) policies and guidance issued by —
(i)   the Office of the First Minister and deputy First Minister;
(ii)   the Department;
(iii)   the Department for Regional Development;
(b) any matters which appear to that person to be relevant."

9.7.2   The Department of the Environment thus retains significant functions. S.1 of the Act says:
"General functions of Department with respect to development of land
(1)   The Department must formulate and co-ordinate policy for securing the orderly and consistent development of land and the planning of that development.
(2)   The Department must—
(a) ensure that any such policy is in general conformity with the regional development strategy."

9.7.3   Draft Strategic Planning Policy Statement (SPPS) – As part of the reform process, the Northern Ireland Assembly published this document in February 2014 for public consultation. When it is published in its final form, the SPPS must be taken into account by planning authorities in the preparation of Local Development Plans (LDPs), but the draft SPPS specifically states that it will not carry any weight or be given any material consideration in its draft form.

9.7.4   The draft SPPS sets out the policy objectives for development in the countryside, which are expected to be reflected in the Local Development Plans that the district councils are to prepare. Those objectives are:

- to manage growth to achieve appropriate and sustainable patterns of development which supports a vibrant rural community;
- to conserve the landscape and natural resources of the rural area and to protect it from excessive, inappropriate or obtrusive development and from the actual or potential effects of pollution;
- to facilitate development which contributes to a sustainable rural economy; and
- to promote high standards in the design, siting and landscaping of development.

9.7.5   District councils may then bring forward development policies on the following basis:

"… local polices and proposals may be brought forward in the LDP for a range of types of development that will contribute to the aims and objectives of this SPPS and wider sustainability objectives as follows:

- **Residential development** including: small scale social and affordable housing development where demonstrable housing need exists; infilling / rounding off of appropriate development clusters / groups; a replacement dwelling; a farm dwelling; a dwelling or conversion housing linked to rural businesses, and a dwelling/temporary caravan or mobile home where there are compelling personal and domestic circumstances.
- **Other types of development** including: farm diversification, agriculture and forestry development; tourism/holiday accommodation; re-use/conversion of existing buildings."

9.7.6   This approach to planning policy reflects the approach adopted in England of outlining a broad strategic policy with little accompanying guidance as to how applications for new dwellings in the countryside are to be assessed. That is left for the new councils to determine within the general framework.

9.7.7   Transition and PPS 21 – There will be a transitional period between the publication of the final SPPS and when the new district councils' local development plans are "adopted, and found to be sound". The draft SPPS proses that PPS 21, with many other PPSs, remain operational in that transitional period.

9.7.8   It will be for the district councils working within the objective of sustainable development and the SPPS to determine their own policies for rural workers' housing.

PREVIOUS ENGLISH GUIDANCE ON AGRICULTURAL DWELLINGS

A.   Circular 11/95: Use of Conditions in Planning Permission

Paragraphs 102 to 105 – Withdrawn with the "launch of the Planning Practice Guidance suite" – taken to be March 2014

Agricultural dwellings
102. Despite planning policies which impose strict controls on new residential development in the open countryside, there may be circumstances where permission is granted to allow a house to be built to accommodate an agricultural or forestry worker on a site where residential development would not normally be permitted. In these circumstances, a condition should be imposed to ensure that the dwellings are kept available for meeting this need – see model condition 45. (see end note 4)

103. It should not be necessary to tie occupation of the dwelling to workers engaged in one specific farm or forestry business even though the needs of that business justified the provision of the dwelling. The model occupancy condition will ensure that the dwelling is kept available to meet the needs of other farm or forestry businesses in the locality if it is no longer needed by the original business, thus avoiding a proliferation of dwellings in the open countryside (see Annex E of PPG7: The Countryside and the Rural Economy for further details about agricultural and forestry dwellings).

104. Local planning authorities will wish to take care to frame agricultural occupancy conditions in such a way as to ensure that their purpose is clear. In particular, they will wish to ensure that the condition does not have the effect of preventing occupation by the dependants of the person defined (the agricultural occupant). (see end note 5)

105. Where an agricultural occupancy condition has been imposed it will not be appropriate to remove it on a subsequent application unless it is shown that the existing need for dwellings for agricultural workers in the locality no longer warrants reserving the house for that purpose. This assessment will be necessary in all cases, including those where the condition was originally inappropriately imposed (Sevenoaks DC v Secretary of State for the Environment and Mr and Mrs Geer (1995) 69 P.& C.R.87). However, the fact that planning permission for a dwelling would in all probability be granted today without an agricultural occupancy condition is a material consideration (Hambleton DC v Secretary of State for the Environment and others [1994] EGCS 202).

End Notes
4. Model condition 45 includes the words " ... limited to a person solely or mainly working, or last working, in the locality in agriculture or forestry ...". "Last working" covers the case both of a person who is temporarily unemployed or of a person who from old age, or illness is no longer able to work. Nor need the words necessarily exclude a person who is engaged in other part-time, or temporary employment, if that person could still be regarded as a farm worker or retired farm worker, or a worker in one of the other specified categories. (Fawcett Properties Ltd v Buckingham County Council [1961] A.C. 636 at pages 671 to 672). A person who last worked in agriculture/forestry but who now works on a permanent basis mainly in non-agricultural/forestry employment, would not satisfy model condition 45.

5. "Dependants" means persons living in family with the person defined and dependent on him (or her) in whole or in part for their subsistence and support (Fawcett Properties Ltd v Buckingham County Council [1961] A.C. 636 at page 671).

Appendix A – Suggested Models of Acceptable Conditions for Use in Appropriate Circumstances – Still in Force

Agricultural Workers' Condition
45. The occupation of the dwelling shall be limited to a person solely or mainly working, or last working, in the locality in agriculture or in forestry, or a widow or widower of such a person, and to any resident dependants (*paragraphs 102-105*).

B: PPS7 – ANNEXE A – WITHDRAWN MARCH 2012

AGRICULTURAL, FORESTRY AND OTHER OCCUPATIONAL DWELLINGS

1. Paragraph 10 of PPS7 makes clear that isolated new houses in the countryside require special justification for planning permission to be granted. One of the few circumstances in which isolated residential development may be justified is when accommodation is required to enable agricultural, forestry and certain other full-time workers to live at, or in the immediate vicinity of, their place of work. It will often be as convenient and more sustainable for such workers to live in nearby towns or villages, or suitable existing dwellings, so avoiding new and potentially intrusive development in the countryside. However, there will be some cases where the nature and demands of the work concerned make it essential for one or more people engaged in the enterprise to live at, or very close to, the site of their work. Whether this is essential in any particular case will depend on the needs of the enterprise concerned and not on the personal preferences or circumstances of any of the individuals involved.

2. It is essential that all applications for planning permission for new occupational dwellings in the countryside are scrutinised thoroughly with the aim of detecting attempts to abuse (e.g. through speculative proposals) the concession that the planning system makes for such dwellings. In particular, it will be important to establish whether the stated intentions to engage in farming, forestry or any other rural-based enterprise, are genuine, are reasonably likely to materialise and are capable of being sustained for a reasonable period of time. It will also be important to establish that the needs of the intended enterprise require one or more of the people engaged in it to live nearby.

Permanent agricultural dwellings
3. New permanent dwellings should only be allowed to support existing agricultural activities on well-established agricultural units, providing:
  (i)   there is a clearly established *existing* functional need (see paragraph 4 below);
  (ii) the need relates to a *full-time* worker, or one who is primarily employed in agriculture and does not relate to a part-time requirement;
  (iii) the unit and the agricultural activity concerned have been established for at least three years, have been profitable for at least one of them, are currently financially sound, and have a clear prospect of remaining so (see paragraph 8 below);
  (iv) the functional need could not be fulfilled by another existing dwelling on the unit, or any other existing accommodation in the area which is suitable and available for occupation by the workers concerned; and

(v) other planning requirements, e.g. in relation to access, or impact on the countryside, are satisfied.

4. A *functional test* is necessary to establish whether it is essential for the proper functioning of the enterprise for one or more workers to be readily available at most times. Such a requirement might arise, for example, if workers are needed to be on hand day and night:

(i) in case animals or agricultural processes require essential care at short notice;

(ii) to deal quickly with emergencies that could otherwise cause serious loss of crops or products, for example, by frost damage or the failure of automatic systems.

5. In cases where the local planning authority is particularly concerned about possible abuse, it should investigate the history of the holding to establish the recent pattern of use of land and buildings and whether, for example, any dwellings, or buildings suitable for conversion to dwellings, have recently been sold separately from the farmland concerned. Such a sale could constitute evidence of lack of agricultural need.

6. The protection of livestock from theft or injury by intruders may contribute on animal welfare grounds to the need for a new agricultural dwelling, although it will not by itself be sufficient to justify one. Requirements arising from food processing, as opposed to agriculture, cannot be used to justify an agricultural dwelling. Nor can agricultural needs justify the provision of isolated new dwellings as retirement homes for farmers.

7. If a functional requirement is established, it will then be necessary to consider the number of workers needed to meet it, for which the scale and nature of the enterprise will be relevant.

8. New permanent accommodation cannot be justified on agricultural grounds unless the farming enterprise is economically viable. A *financial test* is necessary for this purpose, and to provide evidence of the size of dwelling which the unit can sustain. In applying this test (see paragraph 3(iii) above), authorities should take a realistic approach to the level of profitability, taking account of the nature of the enterprise concerned. Some enterprises which aim to operate broadly on a subsistence basis, but which nonetheless provide wider benefits (e.g. in managing attractive landscapes or wildlife habitats), can be sustained on relatively low financial returns.

9. Agricultural dwellings should be of a size commensurate with the established functional requirement. Dwellings that are unusually large in relation to the agricultural needs of the unit, or unusually expensive to construct in relation to the income it can sustain in the long-term, should not be permitted. It is the requirements of the enterprise, rather than those of the owner or occupier, that are relevant in determining the size of dwelling that is appropriate to a particular holding.

10. Local planning authorities may wish to consider making planning permissions subject to conditions removing some of the permitted development rights under part 1 of the Town and Country Planning (General Permitted Development) Order 1995 for development within the curtilage of a dwelling house. For example, proposed extensions could result in a dwelling whose size exceeded what could be justified by the functional requirement, and affect the continued viability of maintaining the property for its intended use, given the income that the agricultural unit can sustain. However, it will

always be preferable for such conditions to restrict the use of specific permitted development rights rather than to be drafted in terms which withdraw all those in a Class (see paragraphs 86-90 of the Annex to DOE Circular 11/95).

11. Agricultural dwellings should be sited so as to meet the identified functional need and to be well-related to existing farm buildings, or other dwellings.

Temporary agricultural dwellings

12. If a new dwelling is essential to support a new farming activity, whether on a newly-created agricultural unit or an established one, it should normally, for the first three years, be provided by a caravan, a wooden structure which can be easily dismantled, or other temporary accommodation. It should satisfy the following criteria:

(i) clear evidence of a firm intention and ability to develop the enterprise concerned (significant investment in new farm buildings is often a good indication of intentions);

(ii) functional need (see paragraph 4 of this Annex);

(iii) clear evidence that the proposed enterprise has been planned on a sound financial basis;

(iv) the functional need could not be fulfilled by another existing dwelling on the unit, or any other existing accommodation in the area which is suitable and available for occupation by the workers concerned; and

(v) other normal planning requirements ,e.g. on siting and access, are satisfied.

13. If permission for temporary accommodation is granted, permission for a permanent dwelling should not subsequently be given unless the criteria in paragraph 3 above are met. The planning authority should make clear the period for which the temporary permission is granted, the fact that the temporary dwelling will have to be removed, and the requirements that will have to be met if a permanent permission is to be granted. Authorities should not normally grant successive extensions to a temporary permission over a period of more than three years, nor should they normally give temporary permissions in locations where they would not permit a permanent dwelling.

Forestry dwellings

14. Local planning authorities should apply the same criteria to applications for forestry dwellings as to those for agricultural dwellings. The other principles in the advice on agricultural dwellings are equally relevant to forestry dwellings. Under conventional methods of forestry management, which can involve the use of a peripatetic workforce, new forestry dwellings may not always be justified, except perhaps to service intensive nursery production of trees.

Other occupational dwellings

15. There may also be instances where special justification exists for new isolated dwellings associated with other rural based enterprises. In these cases, the enterprise itself, including any development necessary for the operation of the enterprise, must be acceptable in planning terms and permitted in that rural location, regardless of the consideration of any proposed associated dwelling. Local planning authorities should apply the same stringent levels of assessment to applications for such new occupational dwellings as they apply to applications for agricultural and forestry workers' dwellings. They should therefore apply the same criteria and principles in paragraphs 3-13 of this Annex, in a manner and to the extent that they are relevant to the nature of the enterprise concerned.

Occupancy conditions

16. Where the need to provide accommodation to enable farm, forestry or other workers to live at or near their place of work has been accepted as providing the special justification required for new, isolated residential development in the countryside, it will be necessary to ensure that the dwellings are kept available for meeting this need for as long as it exists. For this purpose planning permission should be made subject to appropriate occupancy conditions. DOE Circular 11/95 gives further advice and provides model occupancy conditions for agricultural dwellings and for other staff accommodation.

17. Changes in the scale and character of farming and forestry may affect the longer-term requirement for dwellings for which permission has been granted subject to an agricultural or forestry occupancy condition. Such dwellings, and others in the countryside with an occupancy condition attached, should not be kept vacant, nor should their present occupants be unnecessarily obliged to remain in occupation simply by virtue of planning conditions restricting occupancy which have outlived their usefulness. Local planning authorities should set out in LDDs their policy approach to the retention or removal of agricultural and, where relevant, forestry and other forms of occupancy conditions. These policies should be based on an up to date assessment of the demand for farm (or other occupational) dwellings in the area, bearing in mind that it is the need for a dwelling for someone solely, mainly or last working in agriculture or forestry in an area as a whole, and not just on the particular holding, that is relevant in the case of farm or forestry workers' dwellings.

Information and appraisals

18. Planning authorities should be able to determine most applications for occupational dwellings in the countryside, including cases involving the imposition or removal of occupancy conditions, on the basis of their experience and the information provided by the applicant and any other interested parties. If this is not the case, agricultural or other consultants may be able to give a technical appraisal. This should be confined to a factual statement of the agricultural, or other business considerations involved and an evaluation of the specific points on which advice is sought; no recommendation for or against the application should be made.

APPENDIX 2

ENGLISH PLANNING GUIDANCE WITHDRAWN
ON THE INTRODUCTION OF THE NPPF
AND THE LAUNCH OF THE PLANNING PRACTICE GUIDANCE SUITE

Guidance documents cancelled by the National Planning Policy Framework (March 2012) include:
- Planning Policy Statement: *Delivering Sustainable Development* (31 January 2005)
- Planning Policy Guidance 2: *Green Belts* (24 January 1995)
- Planning Policy Statement 3: *Housing* (9 June 2011)
- Planning Policy Statement 7: *Sustainable Development in Rural Areas* (3 August 2004)
- Planning Policy Statement 12: *Local Spatial Planning* (4 June 2008)
- Planning Policy Guidance 18: *Enforcing Planning Control* (20 December 1991)
- Planning Policy Statement 25: *Development and Flood Risk* (29 March 2010)
- Circular 05/2005: *Planning Obligations* (18 July 2005)
- Letter to Chief Planning Officers: *Planning Obligations and Planning Registers* (3 April 2002)
- Letter to Chief Planning Officers: *The Localism Bill* (15 December 2010)

Guidance documents cancelled by launch of the Planning Practice Guidance Suite (6th March 2014) include:
- Circular 22/80 – Development Control and Practice (but not withdrawn for Wales)
- Circular 11/95 – The Use of Conditions in Planning Permissions (1995) – but Appendix A (model conditions) to be retained
- Annex E to PPG7 on Agricultural Permitted Development (1997)
- Circular 03/99 – Planning Requirement in respect of the Use of Non-Mains Sewerage incorporating Septic Tanks in New Development (1999)
- A Farmer's Guide to the Planning System
- Planning Obligations: Practice Guidance (2006)
- Community Infrastructure Levy: Summary (2010)
- Community Infrastructure Levy Guidance: charge setting and charging schedule – procedures (2010)
- Technical Guidance to the National Planning Policy Framework (2012)
- Community Infrastructure Levy Guidance (2013)

ENGLAND – NEW USE CLASS MB
CONVERSION OF AGRICULTURAL BUILDINGS TO DWELLINGS

Class MB
Introduced by Article 5 of
The Town and Country Planning (General Permitted Development)
(Amendment and Consequential Provisions) (England) Order 2014
SI 2014/564

Permitted development

MB. Development consisting of—

(a) **a change of use of a building and any land within its curtilage from use as an agricultural building to a use falling within Class C3 (dwellinghouses) of the Schedule to the Use Classes Order; and**

(b) **building operations reasonably necessary to convert the building referred to in paragraph (a) to a use falling within Class C3 (dwellinghouses) of that Schedule.**

Development not permitted

MB.1. Development is not permitted by Class MB where—

(a) the site was not used solely for an agricultural use, as part of an established agricultural unit—
   (i)   on 20th March 2013;
   (ii) if the site was not in use on that date, when it was last in use; or
   (iii) if the site was brought into use after that date, for ten years before the date the development begins;

(b) the cumulative floor space of the existing building or buildings changing use under Class MB within an established agricultural unit exceeds 450 square metres;

(c) the cumulative number of separate dwellinghouses developed within an established agricultural unit exceeds three;

(d) the site is occupied under an agricultural tenancy, unless the express consent of both the landlord and the tenant has been obtained;

(e) less than one year before the date development begins—
   (i) an agricultural tenancy over the site has been terminated, and
   (ii) the termination was for the purpose of carrying out development under Class MB, unless both the landlord and the tenant have agreed in writing that the site is no longer required for agricultural use;

(f) development under Class A(a) or Class B(a) of Part 6 of this Schedule (agricultural buildings and operations) has been carried out on the established agricultural unit since 20th March 2013, or within 10 years before the date development under Class MB begins, whichever is the lesser;

(g) the development would result in the external dimensions of the building extending beyond the external dimensions of the existing building at any given point;

(h) the development (together with any previous development under Class MB) would result in more than 450 square metres of floor space of building or buildings within an established agricultural unit having changed use under Class MB;

(i) the development under Class MB(b) would consist of building operations other than—
   (i) the installation or replacement of—
       (aa) windows, doors, roofs, or exterior walls, or
       (bb) water, drainage, electricity, gas or other services,
           to the extent reasonably necessary for the building to function as a dwellinghouse; and

(ii) partial demolition to the extent reasonably necessary to carry out building operations allowed by paragraph MB.1(i)(i);

(j) the site is on article 1(5) land;

(k) the site is or forms part of—
    (i)   a site of special scientific interest;
    (ii) a safety hazard area;
    (iii) a military explosives storage area;

(l) the site is, or contains, a scheduled monument;

(m) the building is a listed building.

Conditions

MB.2 (1) Class MB(a) development is permitted subject to the condition that before beginning the development, the developer shall apply to the local planning authority for a determination as to whether the prior approval of the authority will be required as to—

(a) transport and highways impacts of the development,

(b) noise impacts of the development,

(c) contamination risks on the site,

(d) flooding risks on the site, or

(e) whether the location or siting of the building makes it otherwise impractical or undesirable for the building to change from agricultural use to a use falling within Class C3 (dwellinghouses) of the Schedule to the Use Classes Order,

and the provisions of paragraph N of this Part shall apply in relation to any such application.

(2) Class MB(b) development is permitted subject to the condition that before beginning the development, the developer shall apply to the local planning authority for a determination as to whether the prior approval of the authority will be required as to the design or external appearance of the building, and the provisions of paragraph N of this Part shall apply in relation to that application.

(3) Class MB development is permitted subject to the condition that the development shall begin within a period of three years beginning with the date on which—

(a) any prior approval is granted for that development, or

(b) the period of days referred to in paragraph N(9)(c) of this Part expires without the local planning authority notifying the developer as to whether prior approval for that development is given or refused,

whichever is the earlier.

Definitions

"agricultural tenancy" means a tenancy under—

(i) the Agricultural Holdings Act 1986; or

(ii) the Agricultural Tenancies Act 1995;

for the definition of "curtilage" substitute—

" "curtilage" means, for the purposes of Class M, MA or MB only—

(i) the piece of land, whether enclosed or unenclosed, immediately beside or around the agricultural building, closely associated with and serving the purposes of the agricultural building, or

(ii) an area of land immediately beside or around the agricultural building no larger than the land area occupied by the agricultural building,
whichever is the lesser;

"established agricultural unit" means agricultural land occupied as a unit for the purposes of agriculture—
(i) for the purposes of Class M, on or before 3rd July 2012 or for ten years before the date the development begins; or
(ii) for the purposes of Class MA or MB, on or before 20th March 2013 or for ten years before the date the development begins;

THE OTHER PERMITTED CHANGES OF USE FOR AGRICULTURAL BUILDINGS IN ENGLAND: USE CLASSES M AND MA

Class M
Introduced by Article 6 of
The Town and Country Planning (General Permitted Development) (Amendment) (England) Order 2013 SI 2013/1101

Permitted development

M. Development consisting of a change of use of a building and any land within its curtilage from use as an agricultural building to a flexible use falling within either Class A1 (shops), Class A2 (financial and professional services), Class A3 (restaurants and cafes), Class B1 (business), Class B8 (storage or distribution), Class C1 (hotels) or Class D2 (assembly and leisure) of the Schedule to the Use Classes Order.

Development not permitted

M.1 Development is not permitted by Class M if—

(a) the building has not been solely in agricultural use—
   (i) since 3rd July 2012; or
   (ii) for buildings first brought into use after 3rd July 2012, for ten years;
(b) the cumulative floor space of buildings which have changed use under Class M within an original agricultural unit exceeds 500 square metres;
(c) the site is or forms part of a military explosives storage area;
(d) the site is or forms part of a safety hazard area;
(e) the building is a listed building or a scheduled monument.

Conditions

M.2 Development is permitted by Class M subject to the following conditions—

(a) a site which has changed use under Class M may, subject to paragraph M.3, subsequently change use to another use falling within one of the use classes comprising the flexible use.
(b) for the purposes of the Use Classes Order and this Order, after a site has changed use under Class M the site it is to be treated as having a sui generis use;
(c) after a site has changed use under Class M, the planning permissions granted by Class B of Part 41 of Schedule 2 to this Order apply to the building, subject to the following modifications—
   (i) "curtilage" has the meaning given in Class M;
   (ii) any reference to "office building" is to be read as a reference to the building which has changed use under Class M.

M.3 Before changing the use of the site under Class M, and before any subsequent change of use to another use falling within one of the use classes comprising the flexible use, the developer shall—

(a) where the cumulative floor space of the building or buildings which have changed use under Class M within an original agricultural unit does not exceed 150 square metres, provide the following information to the local planning authority—
   (i) the date the site will begin to be used for any of the flexible uses;
   (ii) the nature of the use or uses; and
   (iii) a plan indicating the site and which buildings have changed use;

(b) where the cumulative floor space of the building or buildings which have changed use under Class M within an original agricultural unit exceeds 150 square metres and does not exceed 500 square metres, apply to the local planning authority for a determination as to whether the prior approval of the authority will be required as to—

    (i)   transport and highways impacts of the development;

    (ii) noise impacts of the development;

    (iii) contamination risks on the site; and

    (iv) flooding risks on the site,

and the provisions of paragraph N (procedure for applications for prior approval) shall apply in relation to any such application.

Class MA
Introduced by Article 5 of
The Town and Country Planning (General Permitted Development)
(Amendment and Consequential Provisions) (England) Order 2014
SI 2014/564

Permitted development

MA. Development consisting of a change of use of a building and any land within its curtilage from use as an agricultural building to use as a state-funded school or a registered nursery.

Development not permitted

MA.1 Development is not permitted by Class MA where—

(a) the building was not used solely for an agricultural use, as part of an established agricultural unit—

    (i)   on 20th March 2013;

    (ii) if the building was not in use on that date, when it was last in use; or

    (iii) if the building was brought into use after that date, for ten years before the date development begins;

(b) the cumulative area of—

    (i)   floor space within the existing building or buildings, and

    (ii) land within the curtilage of that building or those buildings,

    changing use under Class MA within an established agricultural unit exceeds 500 square metres;

(c) the site is occupied under an agricultural tenancy, unless the express consent of both the landlord and the tenant has been obtained;

(d) less than one year before the date development begins—

    (i)   an agricultural tenancy over the site has been terminated, and

    (ii) the termination was for the purpose of carrying out development under Class MA,

unless both the landlord and the tenant have agreed in writing that the site is no longer required for agricultural use;

(e) development under Class A(a) or Class B(a) of Part 6 of this Schedule (agricultural buildings and operations) has been carried out on the established agricultural unit since 20th March 2013, or within 10 years before the date development under Class MA begins, whichever is the lesser;

(f) the site is or forms part of—

    (i)   a site of special scientific interest;

    (ii) a safety hazard area; or

    (iii) a military explosives storage area;

(g) the site is, or contains, a scheduled monument;

(h) the building is a listed building.

Conditions

MA.2 Development is permitted by Class MA subject to the following conditions—

(a) the site is to be used as a state-funded school or, as the case may be, as a registered nursery and for no other purpose, including any other purpose falling within Class D1 (non-residential institutions) of the Schedule to the Use Classes Order, except to the extent that the other purpose is ancillary to the primary use of the site as a state-funded school or, as the case may be, as a registered nursery;

(b) after a site has changed use under Class MA, the planning permissions granted by Class B of Part 41 of this Schedule apply to the building, subject to the following modifications—

    (i) "curtilage" has the meaning given in paragraph O of this Part; and

    (ii) any reference to "office building" is to be read as a reference to the building which has changed use under Class MA;

(c) before changing the use of the site under Class MA the developer shall apply to the local planning authority for a determination as to whether the prior approval of the authority will be required as to—

    (i) transport and highways impacts of the development,

    (ii) noise impacts of the development

    (iii) contamination risks on the site,

    (iv) flooding risks on the site, and

    (v) whether the location or siting of the building makes it otherwise impractical or undesirable for the building to change to use as a state-funded school or, as the case may be, a registered nursery,

and the provisions of paragraph N of this Part shall apply in relation to any such application;

(d) development shall begin within a period of three years beginning with the date on which—

    (i) any prior approval is granted for that development, or

    (ii) the period of days referred to in paragraph N(9)(c) of this Part expires without the local planning authority notifying the developer as to whether prior approval for that development is given or refused,

whichever is the earlier.

FLOW CHART FOR ASSESSING TAN 6 PROPOSALS
(Welsh Government Practice Guidance at 3.4)

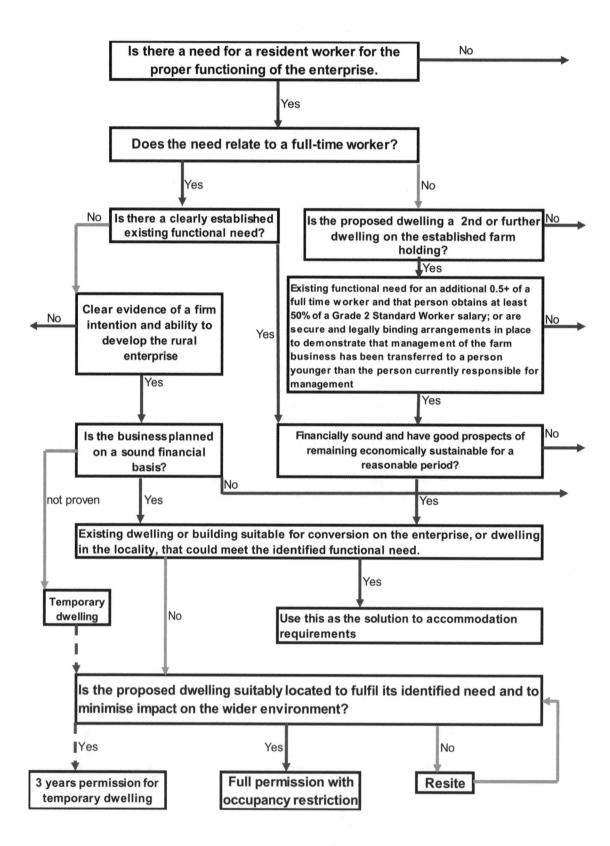

POSSIBLE FRAMEWORK FOR A TAN 6
RURAL ENTERPRISE DWELLING APPRAISAL

Robust evidence is expected to support any application for such a dwelling. An appraisal is to accompany each application with:

"information sufficient to enable the planning authority to make a full and effective assessment."

This framework for such an appraisal is offered here as a prompt to thought, not as an exhaustive or universal model. Reference should be made to section 7.5 of this paper for further details on all items.

Where the LPA has someone to advise on such applications it has been found useful to discuss the proposed appraisal with them.

HEADINGS AND ISSUES

The Functional Test

Provide evidence of whether there is a need for a resident worker for the proper functioning of the enterprise. This is driven by the character and management of the business, not personal preferences or circumstances.

Note – there will be particular scrutiny if there are already dwellings on site:

Describe those aspects of the operation and management of the enterprise which require the presence of a resident worker(s).

It is described as "primarily concerned with the management of risk within the operations of an enterprise" so consider:
- identifying potential emergency incidents which require a day and night presence
- unexpected situations that might arise requiring the worker(s) to be on hand outside of normal working hours for the particular enterprise
- how providing immediate attention in this way this might answer threats to the viability of the enterprise

Such issues might include:
- adverse animal welfare – such as where immediate, regular and often unpredictable care over much of the year is required to safeguard:
  - the specific welfare of livestock and offspring in breeding programmes, lambing, calving or foaling conditions or
  - the more general welfare of animals housed in buildings either permanently or for protracted periods, for example in intensive livestock units, stud and livery stables, or commercial kennels.
- crop or product quality – such as where the productive processes or the quality of crops and products are dependent upon the maintenance and security of controlled environments using automated systems, such as in protected cropping horticulture and intensive livestock units.
- Why can adequate surveillance not be achieved through remote means such as CCTV and temperature and other environmental sensors?
- health and safety consequences
- commercial viability – such as where the lack of 24-hour on-site supervision might prejudice the commercial viability of a business, for example at a large established livery yard.

– where the delivery of specialist services is required outside normal hours and where timeliness of response is important;

Identify any changes in the circumstances of the enterprise which have given rise to the requirement for the presence of a resident worker(s)

Where a second dwelling is sought to transfer of the management of an established farm:
- assess the benefits of a transfer of farm management to the younger generation.
- shown that this purpose cannot be met in another way.

The Time Test
Provide evidence of the enterprise's labour requirement for the worker requiring the dwelling. This is to show that there is a substantive need.

Assess the labour requirements of the enterprise. This is to be based on standardised calculations using a standard man day of 8 hours with a full time worker providing 275 such days or 2,200 hours, allowing 15-20 per cent on top of the calculation for general maintenance, repairs and management.

There are three different thresholds for this:
- a new dwelling will ordinarily require a full-time worker
- a second or further dwelling on an established farm will need at least a half time worker. This recognises such situations as where the existing full-time workforce, probably a single individual, cannot effectively meet all the functional needs of the farm enterprise but the shortfall does not justify a second full-time worker. The extra half worker would enable the essential functional needs of the enterprise regularly arising over most of the year to be shared and thereby addressed effectively helping with either or both of:
  • long anti-social hours are involved
  • where it would be unsafe for a single worker to undertake specific tasks.
- The need for a significant proportion of the additional worker's time needs to be based on the essential functional requirements of the agricultural enterprise such as calving or lambing and not simply providing administrative or maintenance support.
- where the extra farm dwelling is needed for the transfer of the majority control of the farm, the worker must be critical to the successful operation of the farm

Indicate the component parts of the enterprise and the amount of time apportioned to each part.

Are there other answers? Consider alternative operational and management strategies available to the enterprise

The Financial Test
As this test is drafted in two parts:
- provide evidence of the economic sustainability of the enterprise justifying the dwelling, over a five year period.
- identify the size of dwelling that the enterprise can sustain, ensuring that the size of the dwelling is commensurate with its functional need and financial justification.

Financial Performance – Does the business have a reasonable prospect of providing a market return for all operators for their management and manual labour inputs, including the job for which the rural enterprise dwelling is being sought, for at least five years from the anticipated completion of the proposed development? Set out:

- details of the actual and/or projected financial performance of the enterprise (accounts, financial statements or business plans). Will it fund its trading?
- assess their implications in terms of the proposal.

An existing business should give financial performance over at least three years, showing:
- enterprise income
- costs of production
- net profit
- the balance between assets and liabilities

Will that provide a return to unpaid labour (at least at the statutory minimum wage) and support the dwelling?

If it is a new enterprise, set out a business plan.
- is it endorsed by a bank or other third party?
- show sensitivity testing for risks.

Will it Pay for the Dwelling? – What size of dwelling is warranted by the requirements of the enterprise?
- give an "indicative build cost" for the dwelling
- will the profit from the enterprise pay for either the finance for borrowing for the dwelling or a modest return on personal investment in it.

It is understood that in practice some LPAs will expect the dwelling to be no more than 180m² and apply a rate of 2.5 per cent.

The Other Dwellings Test
Identify whether there is an existing dwelling or building suitable for conversion on the enterprise or dwelling in the locality that could meet the identified functional need.

What existing dwellings are associated with the rural enterprise (location, occupancy etc)? Are any buildings available and suitable for conversion?
Note – if the business has an existing dwelling occupied by a person not delivering an essential functional input to the enterprise that will not, in itself, be sufficient justification for an additional dwelling.

This may need a review of property websites for dwellings on the market in the necessary area but:
- these might not be suitable for the identified need
- these may be uneconomic propositions
- shortholds are unlikely to offer sufficient security.

Are other recent TAN 6 permissions evidence that there are no other relevant properties?

Other Normal Planning Requirements Test
Reviewing the ordinary requires of the planning regime regarding design, sustainability and access, demonstrate that the dwelling is suitably designed and located to
- fulfil its identified need
  • relating closely to the activities justifying it
  • not be isolated or encouraging farm fragmentation
- minimise impact on the wider environment.
  • not to be too prominent in the landscape
  • how will ground and surface water be handled?
  • can power and heat be generated on-site?

APPENDIX 7

LEGISLATION, CASES AND POLICY DOCUMENTS
LEGISLATION

United Kingdom
Acts
Government of Wales Act 2006
Wales Act 1998
Inheritance Tax Act 1984

Statutory Instruments
Business Protection from Misleading Marketing Regulations 2008 SI 2008/1276
Consumer Protection from Unfair Trading Regulations 2008 SI 2008/1277

Great Britain
Acts
Caravan Sites and Control of Development Act 1960

England, Wales and Northern Ireland
Acts
National Parks and Access to the Countryside Act 1949

England and Wales
Acts
Localism Act 2011
Planning Act 2008
Planning and Compulsory Purchase Act 2004
Agricultural Tenancies Act 1995
Planning and Compensation Act 1991
Planning (Listed Buildings and Conservation Areas) Act 1990
Town and Country Planning Act 1990
Agricultural Holdings Act 1986
Town and Country Planning Act 1947
Law of Property Act 1925

Statutory Instruments
England and Wales
Community Infrastructure Levy Regulations 2010 SI 2010/948
National Assembly for Wales (Transfer of Functions) Order 1999 SI 1999/672
Town and Country Planning (General Permitted Development) Order 1995 SI 1995/418

England
The Town and Country Planning (General Permitted Development) (Amendment and Consequential Provisions) (England) Order 2014 SI 2014/564
The Town and Country Planning (General Permitted Development) (Amendment) (England) Order 2014 SI 2013/1101

Scotland
Act
Planning Etc (Scotland) Act 2006
National Parks (Scotland) Act 2000
Town and Country Planning (Scotland) Act 1997
Planning (Listed Buildings and Conservation Areas) (Scotland) Act 1997

Northern Ireland
Acts
Planning Act (Northern Ireland) 2011
Interpretation Act (Northern Ireland) 1954

Statutory Instruments
Planning (Use Classes) Order (Northern Ireland) 2004
Planning (Amendment) (Northern Ireland) Order 2003 (NI 8)
Planning (General Development) Order (Northern Ireland) 1993
Planning (Northern Ireland) Order 1991 (NI 11) 1991/1220

POLICY STATEMENTS

England
National Planning Policy Framework (2012) – NPPF
Planning Practice Guidance Rural Housing (March 2014)
Appendix A to Circular 11/95
Use of Planning Conditions (March 2014)

Wales
Planning Policy Wales (2014)
Technical Advice Note 6 – Planning for Sustainable Rural Communities (2010) – TAN 6
Practice Guidance – Rural Enterprise Dwellings (2011)
Circular 16/2014 – The Use of Planning Conditions in Development Management (2014)

Scotland
Scottish Planning Policy 2014
National Planning Framework 3 (2014)
Circular 3/2012 – Planning Obligations and Good Neighbour Agreements
Letter from Scottish Government's Director and Chief Planner to local authority Heads
    of Planning – 4th November 2011 on occupancy conditions
Letter from Scottish Government's Director and Chief Planner to local authority Heads
    of Planning – 5th July 2011 on S.75 Planning Obligations
Letter from Scottish Government's Director and Chief Planner to Heads of Planning –
    3rd November 2009 on housing for retired tenant farmers
Circular 4/1998 – The Use of Conditions in Planning Permissions
Addendum to Circular 4/1998 – Model Planning Conditions (1999)

Northern Ireland
Regional Development Strategy (2012)
Planning Policy Statement 21 – Sustainable Development in the Countryside (2010)

CASES

Agriculture Sector (Wales) Bill Reference by the Attorney General for England and
    Wales [2014] UKSC 43
Atkinson (see HMRC v Atkinson)
Cherkley Campaign Ltd, R (on the application of) v Mole Valley District Council & Anor
    [2014] EWCA Civ 567
City of Edinburgh Council v Secretary of State for Scotland and Others [1997] UKHL
    38; [1998] 1 All ER 174; [1997] 1 WLR 1447

JR Cussons & Son v Secretary of State for Communities and Local Government and North York Moors National Park Authority [2008] EWHC 443 (Admin)

Embleton Parish Council & Anor, R (on the application of) v Gaston [2013] EWHC 3631 (Admin)

Epping Forest District Council v Secretary of State for Transport, Local Government & the Regions [2005] EWHC 424 (Admin)

Fawcett Properties Ltd v Buckingham County Council [1961] AC 636

Federated Estates Limited v Secretary of State for the Environment and Gillingham Borough Council [1983] JPL 812

Ford v Secretary of State for Communities and Local Government and North Somerset District Council [2007] EWCH 252 (Admin)

Fuller v Secretary of State for the Environment [1988] 01 EG 55

HMRC v Atkinson [2011] UTUK (TCC) FTC/61/2010

Keen v Secretary of State for the Environment and Aylesbury Vale District Council [1996] 71 P&CR 543

Lliw Valley Borough Council v Secretary of State for Wales and Evans [1993] JPL 673

McPhail v Greensmith [1993] 2 EGLR 228 CA

Millbank (Exors of) v Secretary of State for the Environment [1990] JPL 518; [1991] 61 P&CR 16

Newbury District Council v Secretary of State for the Environment [1981] AC 578

Normanton, Earl of v Giles [1980] 1 WLR 28 HL

Pyx Granite Co Ltd v Ministry of Housing and Local Government [1960] AC 260

Re Martins' Application [1989] 57 P&CR 119

Re Truman, Hanbury, Buxton and Co Ltd's Application [1956] 1 QB 261

Rasbridge UKUT [2012] 246 LP 40 2010

R (on the application of Forge Field Society) v Sevenoaks District Council [2014] EWHC

Shortt v Secretary of State for Communities and Local Government [2014] EWHC 2480 (Admin)

Thakeham Village Action v Horsham District Council [2014] EWHC 67

Wealden District Council v Secretary of State for the Environment [1988] 08 EG 112; [1986 JPL 753